Business Families of Ludhiana

Business Families of Ludhiana

Chief Editor
Dr. K.N.S. Kang

PCTE
Punjab College of Technical Education
Ludhiana

NEW NC CENTURY
New Century Publications
Delhi India

New Century Publications
34, Gujranwala Town, Part-2,
Delhi - 110 009 INDIA
Tel.: 27247805, 27138192
Fax: +91-11-27464774
E-mail: indiatax@del2.vsnl.net.in

First Published 2003

ISBN: 81-7708-052-0

Published by New Century Publications and printed at Singhal Print Media, Delhi -110 007

PRINTED IN INDIA

About the Book

The present business environment is vastly different from what it was a decade ago. In the wake of liberalisation and globalisation, domestic industry has to gear itself for the new challenges of global competitiveness and quality. Sustainable growth, social justice and ethical issues are the other challenges that need to be met.

Ludhiana, the industrial hub of Punjab, stands out as a symbol of hard work and entrepreneurial skills of its citizens. The phenomenal growth of industry in Ludhiana is emulated as a role model across India.

The present book places on record the achievements of Ludhiana's entrepreneurs in the industrialisation of India in general and that of Punjab in particular. It documents and consolidates the contribution of enterprising families of Ludhiana in placing this city on the industrial map of India. The book would prove useful for students of management and commerce, business executives and market analysts. It will also serve as a catalyst for present and prospective entrepreneurs who will get an insight into the rough and tough world of business and industry.

Editor's Profile

Dr. K.N.S. Kang, Director, Punjab College of Technical Education, is an Electrical Engineer with Post-graduation in Business Management and Doctorate in Marketing Management. He has worked as an Assistant Professor in the Department of Business Management, Punjab Agricultural University, Ludhiana. He has twelve years of teaching and industry experience to his credit. Dr. Kang's areas of interest include marketing, international business and advertising management. He is consultant to various industrial houses in Ludhiana and a member of several committees and associations.

Punjab College of Technical Education (PCTE)

Started in August 1999, PCTE provides technical and management education to the students by conducting Master of Business Administration (MBA), Master of Computer Applications (MCA), Bachelor of Business Administration (BBA) and Bachelor of Computer Applications (BCA) programmes at its campus located at Baddowal, Ferozepur Road, Ludhiana.

As part of its endeavour to provide quality education, PCTE organises students' interaction with industry on a regular basis. Through research assignments, students are required to interact with industry through field visits to enable them to gain insight into the working of various industrial units. Eminent speakers are also invited from industry and academic institutions to share their experiences and thoughts with students and faculty members. PCTE also stimulates all-round development of personality by organising various co-curricular activities for the students.

Acknowledgements

We wish to place on record our gratitude to the members of the business families of Ludhiana who readily extended their support by way of providing material for this book. Thanks are also due to the key personnel of the companies covered in this volume who spared valuable time to attend to the PCTE team that visited them for collecting material and supporting information about their respective organisations. Without their co-operation this compilation would not have been possible.

Punjab College of Technical Education
Ludhiana

Preface

The state of Punjab is characterised by the indomitable spirit of its people. Contemporary Ludhiana stands out as a symbol of this spirit, hard work and entrepreneurial skills of its citizens. No surprise, Ludhiana is emulated as a model of industrial progress across India. Business acumen is an inherent attribute of its people, old and young.

The sprawling city of Ludhiana, occupying an area of 3762 sq. km., is inhabited by approximately 35 lakh people with a literacy rate of 67.29 per cent.

The city has two Focal Points, three Industrial Areas (A, B and C), one Urban Estate (Industrial) and three Rural Industrial Estates, developed by the State Government.

India, though having a rich cultural heritage, is a poor country in terms of per capita earning and the standard of living of its citizens. This unsatisfactory state of affairs is largely attributable to lack of industrialisation and heavy dependence on agriculture.

Ludhiana has broken away from its agricultural bias and opted for industrialisation. Choosing the fast track to development through industrialisation, it set about building *temples of modern India* as envisioned by Pandit Jawaharlal Nehru. Cities like Tirupur (hosiery), Khurja (ceramics), Farukhabad (glass) have benefited immensely from the *clustering approach*. Ludhiana did not opt for *clustering approach* in the strict sense of the term. Resultantly, present day Ludhiana is a leader in the field of hosiery, bicycles and bicycle components, and hand tools. There is also a significant presence of textile, steel, tyre and tube, and sewing machine industries. Service industry is the latest to establish a base in Ludhiana.

The present business environment is vastly different from

what it was a decade ago. In the wake of liberalisation and globalisation, domestic business and industry has to gear itself for the new challenges of global competitiveness and quality. Sustainable growth, social justice and ethical issues are the other challenges that need to be met.

Ludhiana, the industrial hub of Punjab, stands out as a symbol of hard work and entrepreneurial skills of its citizens. The phenomenal growth of industry in Ludhiana is emulated as a role model across India.

The present book places on record the achievements of Ludhiana's entrepreneurs in the industrialisation of India in general and that of Punjab in particular. It documents and consolidates the contribution of enterprising families of Ludhiana in placing this city on the industrial map of India.

This book is the result of the challenge taken up by the Punjab College of Technical Education to compile essential information about the prominent business/industrial families of Ludhiana to inspire the new generation of entrepreneurs and business managers. A list of business/industrial families was prepared, framework for information collection was drawn up, and teams of Faculty members constituted to start the project. The period that followed was one of hectic activity. Material started flowing in. It had to be organised and computerised. Back-ups were prepared, extensive editing was done and discussions extending to several hours took place to get the material ready for printing. In spite of various road blocks, the work has finally seen the light of the day.

We believe that this compilation will serve multiple purposes. Firstly, it will provide the prospective entrepreneurs (including our own students) the necessary inspiration to venture into the rough and tumble world of business and industry. Secondly, it places on record the contribution of enterprising families to the development of not only Ludhiana but also of Punjab and India. Thirdly, it provides us at PCTE with a feedback to extend the coverage of the business and industrial families to make it more comprehensive. Lastly, it will spread awareness beyond the northern region of India as to how Ludhiana achieved its prime glory as the nucleus of business and industrial activity in Punjab.

March 2003

K.N.S. Kang
Director
Punjab College of Technical Education
Ludhiana

The PCTE Team

Chief Editor

Dr. K.N.S. Kang, Director

Editorial Team

Col. N.K. Mohindar

Sandhir Sharma

Samarjit Kaur

Ashish Pillai

Contributors

Aarti Steels Limited	Atul Grover and Samarjit Kaur
AVON Cycles Limited	Gautam Bansal
Bhogal Group of Companies	Mandeep K. Sodhi
Eastman Industries Limited	Sukhjinder Bath
FMI Limited	Jagdeep Ghai, Sushil Sandhu and Jaswinder Kaur
G.S. Auto International Limited	Khushdeep Dharni
The Hero Group	Namita
Hindustan Cycle and Tube Ltd.	Sukhjinder Bath
Malwa Group of Companies	Arunesh Garg and Sandhir Sharma
Metro Tyres Limited	Arunesh Garg
Nahar Group of Companies	Pallavi Dawra
Ralson India Limited	Deepa Mangala
Shreyans Group	Arunesh Garg and Sandhir Sharma
Upper India Steels	Kawal Deep and Sandhir Sharma
Vardhman	Manveen Kaur Saini

Special Thanks

Arunesh Garg

Pavitar Parkash Singh

Contents

1

Aarti Steels Limited

Introduction: Indian Steel Industry

India is the tenth largest producer of steel in the world, but its per capita consumption is one of the lowest. The industry has been going through difficult times for the last five years due to overcapacity, poor demand growth, and diminishing margins. Consumption grew by a surprisingly 7.6% in FY-01. But it slowed down in FY-02. With over-capacity in the range of 1million ton per annum, difficult times are expected to continue for the industry as a whole. Price trend is also expected to remain weak.

Exports, that had been strong during 1999-2000, have been adversely affected due to the imposition of anti-dumping duties by the US. The difficult times have prompted the industry to restructure and improve operational efficiencies. Difficult times have also resulted in changes in the way steel is being marketed across the country. The customer is emerging as the king. The industry also embraced Internet enthusiastically, however, the enthusiasm has waned in recent times.

Globally, there is a move to cut production capacity with a view to reduce overcapacity, boost steel prices, and improve the fortunes of the steel industry.

Recent quota restriction imposed by US on Korean and Japanese steel has added to the problems of Indian Steel producers, because diversion of steel from USA may lead it straight to Indian Markets. The world steel market in 2001 moved largely downhill, with volume and prices sinking rapidly over the year until early 2002. The US steel market volumes retreated as did shipments, and prices collapsed.

Excess global and US capacity is a very serious problem. Looking back to the mid-1990s, the global steel industry has suffered the following setbacks:

- In 1995, a *pricing* "death spiral" on the world steel export market when the global economy was rising.
- In 1998, a "death spiral" when the global economy was stagnant after the *Asian financial crisis*.
- In 2000, a "death spiral" when the global economy was *booming*.
- In the second half of 2001, after a moderate recovery in the first half of the year, a *renewed price collapse*.

Steel: Production in Public and Private Sectors

(in million tonnes)

Year	Public sector	Private sector	Total
1991-92	6.97 (48.6%)	7.36 (51.4%)	14.33
1992-93	7.47 (49.2%)	7.73 (50.8%)	15.20
1993-94	7.80 (51.3%)	7.40 (48.7%)	15.20
1994-95	8.20 (46%)	9.62 (54%)	17.82
1995-96	8.76 (41%)	12.64 (59%)	21.40
1996-97	8.53 (37.6%)	14.19 (62.4%)	22.72
1997-98	8.55 (37.8%)	14.02 (62.1%)	22.57
1998-99	9.91 (41.6%)	13.91 (58.4%)	23.82
1999-2000	11.86 (44.78%)	14.62 (55.22%)	26.48

Note: Figures in brackets indicate % share.

Impact of Liberalisation on Steel Industry

Even before the economic liberalisation of the 1990s, a few sectors of the Iron and Steel industry were liberalised. Sponge iron was delicensed in the mid-80s; as a result, this sector today ranks only second to Mexico in production.

Similarly, the pig iron industry was delicensed and opened to private sector, to meet the shortage of this vital product for the foundry and the mini-blast furnace units.

The major impetus for growth in this sector came with the economic liberalisation of 1991. The industry was delicensed and opened for private participation; price and distribution controls were removed; "iron and steel" was placed in the high priority list for automatic approval of Foreign Direct Investment; and Import-Export procedures were streamlined. Nineteen major steel plants were sanctioned in the private sector, involving an investment of about 300 billion and capacity generation of 13 million tonnes. Several of these projects have already come up, while others are in various stages of completion. These include Jindal Vijayanagar Steel, Essar Steel Ltd., Lloyds Steel Ltd., Jindal Strips Ltd., Prakash Industries Ltd., Ispat Industries Ltd. and Southern Iron and Steel Co. Ltd.

Steel Exports

Government has set up the Steel Exporter's Forum as an interactive body of major exporters of steel and various ministries, to promote exports. Exports of iron and steel products touched an all time high of 3.4 million tonnes in 1997-98 fetching foreign exchange of over Rs. 29.37 billion.

It is argued that the industry's condition was self-inflicted. Steel production rose to excessive levels in early 2000 and was never cut back sufficiently to positively impact the global supply and demand balance. To sum up, the steel industry's main problem was the recurring tendency to overproduce over the steel cycle, when the market was rising. This, coupled with the failure to cut back output fast enough when the market was weakening, resulted in pricing spirals from 1995 to 2001. It is estimated that global demand will grow 2.2 – 3.0 percent per annum compounded during this decade.

Exports of Iron and Steel

Year	Qty. in million tonnes	Value in Rs. billion
1994-95	2.45	17.18
1995-96	2.80	22.75
1996-97	2.70	23.96
1997-98	3.03	29.37
1998-99	2.39	25.09
1999-2000 (revised)	2.67	26.04

Second major factor which increases the hope of revival of steel industry is that world export prices have rallied in the past few months. There are indications that the current rally may sustain through 2003. There are now adequate barriers in place to prevent unethical trade in steel and overproduction. However there is a word of caution, investment in the steel industry should be controlled and closed capacities should not be revived. Considering the various favourable factors, it is likely that the steel industry is set to re-live its golden era.

Aarti Group: The Profile

Background and Historical Perspective

Before launching Aarti Steels Ltd., Mittal's were into the cycle parts business. They had four companies for manufacturing cycle parts:

1. Behl Industries Pvt. Ltd.
2. S.N. Gandhi & Sons.

3. Deepak Enterprises.
4. Sunflower.

Unfortunately, these companies incurred huge losses which resulted in their shift from the cycle parts business into steel business under the name of Aarti Group.

Sohan Lal Mittal and Shiv Parshad Mittal started Aarti Steels Limited in the year 1977 with an initial investment of approximately Rs. 25 lakhs. They started the group with approximately 30 employees. Their initial product was Iron Rod with a turnover of about Rs.55 lakhs. Their Registered Office is at G.T Road, Miller Ganj, Ludhiana.

Incorporation and Integration

The Aarti Group, which was incorporated in 1977 in the name of Aarti Steels Ltd., achieved an annual turnover of approximately Rs. 367 crores in the year 2001-02 and had a workforce of over 2000 personnel.

In 1979 the company started its first rolling mill and followed it up with a massive programme of vertical and horizontal integration to add various facilities in quick succession. They commissioned Wire Rod Rolling Mill (1982-83), Induction Furnaces (1985-86), Oxygen Plant (1989), Steel Wire Drawing Unit (1991), Tyre Bead Wire Unit (1993) and Electric Arc Furnace (1995)

Aarti Steels Ltd. has also got a mini steel plant with a capacity of 1.25 lac tonnes per annum. This steel plant is the most modern composite plant having 30M.T.EBT (Eccentric Bottom Taping), UHP, EAF (Electric Arc Furnace) with an equal capacity of Laddle Refining and 6/11 m radius three strand continuous casting and other balancing equipment. The R&D set up of the company is well equipped.

Aarti Steels Ltd. manufactures a wide range of products in carbon, spring steel and low alloy steels, which are used in the automobile Industry. Constant upgradation of technology is on top of the agenda of the company. Most modern Electromagnetic Stirring facilities at stage one of modernisation have been installed for quality upgradation on continuous casting machine "26". Continuous Rolling Mill and Vacuum Degassing arrangements were installed in the year 2001.

Exports

The wire division of the company has also ventured into export, and expects a good response because of its acclaimed quality and better service. ISO-9002 is successfully implemented in all the group units.

Social Role

The group is also running a hospital, besides a theatre, at Ludhiana.

Diversification

To expand its identity beyond steel, the company decided to diversify into textile industry. In 1994 it set up Aarti International Ltd., Ludhiana, a 100% export-oriented unit (EOU), for spinning of cotton yarn. It was granted a licence by Government of India for installing 50,000 spindles and 2000 rotors. The company installed 28,224 spindles in the first phase.

Aarti International started construction of its plant in September 1995. This unit started commercial production with effect from November 18, 1996. It later on added another set of 28,080 spindles at same location, which came into commercial production from November 18, 2000.

Family Tree

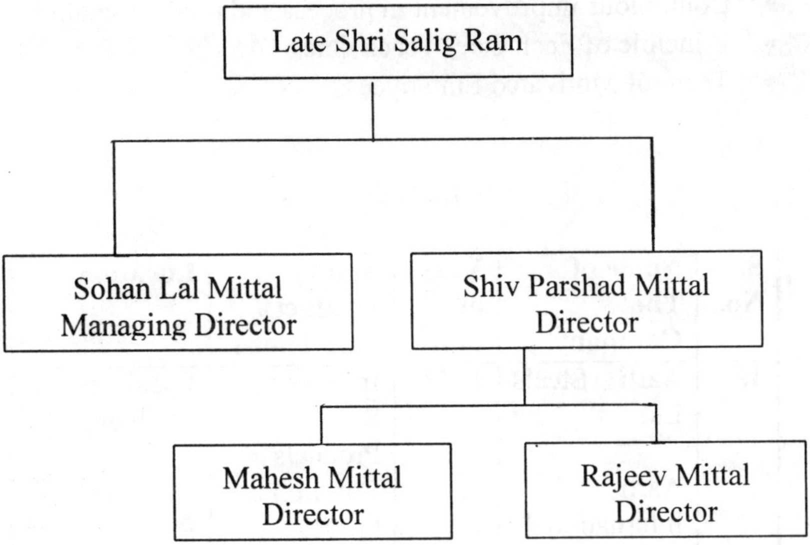

Competitors

The main competitors of Aarti Steels Limited are Upper India Steel Ltd., Modern Steels Limited and Vardhman Special Steels.

Awards and Certifications

Aarti steels limited has been a regular recipient of the ***Rashtriya Sammaan Patra*** from 1994-95 to 1998-99.

The company is ISO 9002 certified (Det Norske Veritas Quality System Certificate).

Quality Policy

Aarti Steels Ltd. is committed to deliver products and services to the entire satisfaction of customers through:

- Quality Management Systems.
- Up-gradation of Technology as per process requirement.
- Continuous improvement in process and product quality.
- Principle of Each One- Teach One.
- Team of Motivated Employees.

Products/Services

S. No.	Name of The Company	Year of Start	Main Products/ Operations	Location
1.	Aarti Steels Ltd.	1977	Iron And Steel Products	Focal Point, Ludhiana
2.	Aarti International Ltd.	1996	Cotton Yarn (100% EOU)	Chandigarh Road, Ludhiana
3.	Salig Ram Shiv Prasad	N.A.	Consign-ment Agency (TISCO)	Focal Point, Ludhiana
4.	Aarti Palace	N.A.	Cinema Hall	Ferozepur Road, Ludhiana

Future Plans

Aarti Steels Ltd. has plans on anvil to establish mini blast furnace in Orissa by the year 2004.

Face to Face with Mr. Shiv Prasad Mittal, Director

Mr. Shiv Prasad Mittal, Director, Aarti Group, responding to the query that to whom he attributed the success of his business said that he considered it as a team effort of two brothers, their sons, and all the staff. "We believe in *Karam hi puja hai.* Success is the result of hard work, innovation, initiative and team work. Our main competitive strength is that we work within our own resources and don't believe in borrowing finance from outside", says Mr. Mittal. Using orthodox approach and not indulging in unethical practices, are the weaknesses of the group according to the Mittals. Mr. Mittal said sarcastically that they lagged behind because they could not deceive people. They have not made any public issue, and are working with their internal sources of finance only.

Regarding the future operational plans , he said that they were planning to set up Blast Furnaces. But these could not be set up in Punjab because of shortage of raw material. "They need to be set up in areas like Chattisgarh where raw material is cheap and readily available", said Mr. Mittal. When he was asked to rate the performance of government in a support role for industry he said that the growth of industry depended on many factors like government policies and growth oriented incentives. For positive growth, proper environment should be there and if it was present, India would definitely grow.

When asked about the competition from low cost firms of China, Mr. Mittal said that local industry was not worried about these threats. Competition was expected from the new technology of Blast Furnace projects, which convert iron into steel directly. Due to lack of iron and coal mines this new technology Blast Furnace was not commercially viable in Punjab. The ideal locations for these units are in Orissa & Chattisgarh. These furnaces would produce steel in large quantities posing a threat for survival of the steel industries in Punjab. But still we have to be competitive whatever may be the case. As mentioned earlier, there is competition from whole of the globe, not only China. Competition is always good for the development of any company so it should be taken positively. If Indian firms are venturing out to other countries, i.e. exporting the products and competing in the world market, then why can't we compete in our own country. To face competition one has to be cost effective and maintain good quality. Globalization is both a threat and opportunity for Indian firms. If the quality of the product is good only then survival would be possible. We should be cost effective in our operations. The main thrust should be on optimum utilization of resources like men, machine and market.

Talking about Information Technology, he said that IT had helped a lot in the business ,but the company was not into IT ventures as such. IT has helped by making all the information available readily and in time. Earlier it used to take very long for preparing Balance Sheet, but with the help of IT the same can be prepared almost daily.

Regarding the criticality of human resource management as compared to other functional areas such as Marketing, Finance, Production, he said that so far as human resources were concerned, they are very important for any concern. In fact they are the most valuable resource in any organization. They are pervasive in all the functional areas and in day-to-day working of business. At every step there was a need for good people to have good quality products.

Although all the functional areas of a concern are very important, for steel industry in particular, human resource management and Quality management are more important. Quality of product should be par excellence for success of any business. Unless quality of product is good, nothing is going to work well. Feedback of customers is a measure of the quality of the product. One can judge the degree of success on the basis of this feedback, which is indeed very important for us.

It is the top most responsibility of every individual to look after and take care of his society. Every business should be aware of its responsibility towards the society. He further added, "We are also trying to fulfil our social responsibilities in a number of ways. We are running a charitable hospital, **Deepak Hospital,** at Sarabha Nagar. We organize vaccination camps every month there. In Nov. 2001, around 2400 people were vaccinated free of cost for "Hepatitis B."

Data Sheet

Year of Start	1977
Main Products/Operations	Melting Secondary Refining Casting Shaping Tyre Bead Wire Galvanized Wire Patenting/WetDrawing Machine Product Mix-Steel Product Mix-Wires Cotton Yarn
Total Turnover	Rs. 367 cr.
Domestic Turnover	Rs. 324 cr.
Foreign Turnover	Rs. 43 cr.
Certifications	ISO 9002 (Det Norske Veritas Quality System Certificate)
Stock Exchange Listings	Nil
New Ventures	Nil
Major Collaborations	Nil
Flagship Company	Aarti Steels Ltd.
Domestic Market	All over India
Foreign Markets	Srilanka, Taiwan, China, Singapore, Bangladesh, Turkey, Korea, Egypt, Belgium, Malaysia, Russia

2

AVON Cycles Limited

AVON Group: The Profile

Background and Historical Perspective

One among pioneers in Bicycle Industry in India with a strong presence in the world market., AVON Cycles Limited is based at Ludhiana. The group was founded by three Pahwa brothers: Mr. Hans Raj Pahwa, Mr. Jagat Singh Pahwa and Mr. Sohan Lal Pahwa. The unit started manufacturing forks as a small scale industry in 1952. Today the company is a major player in bicycle and bicycle parts in the large scale sector.

The company's head office and manufacturing units are located in Ludhiana, a bustling industrial city located in the state of Punjab, the Bicycle capital of the world. AVON Cycles comprises of four units. Established half a century ago, AVON today is a household name. Consistently providing the common man with his means of transport at affordable prices, the house of AVON has contributed significantly in satisfying his need for mobility in a pollution-free and user-friendly manner.

Each bicycle made by the company is a testimony to top quality craftsmanship of its committed work force and is recognised for unchallenged quality standards and durability for over five decades. No wonder bicycle parts products by AVON are certified by ISI. Also, AVON is the only manufacturer of bicycles in India certified by ISI. AVON celebrated its 50 years of existence in 2002.

Present Family Structure

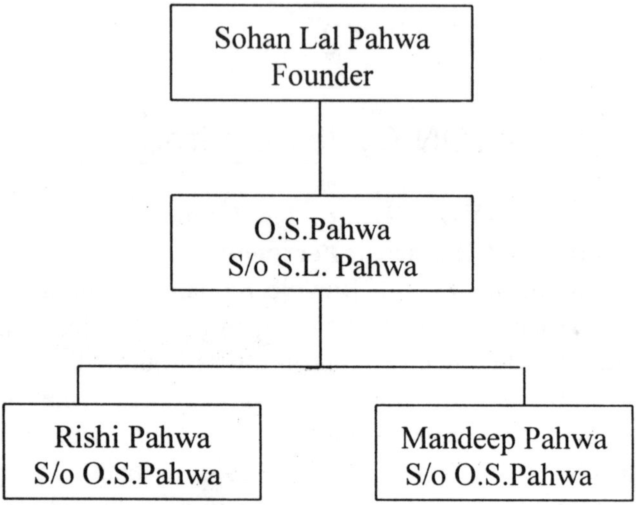

Incorporation and Integration

The group was incorporated in 1952 with an initial investment of Rs.50,000/- and started manufacturing bicycle forks. The turnover today has reached a staggering Rs. 600 crores. AVON Cycles Limited has four divisions:

Division	Location	Product	Turnover (Rs.)
Unit – 1	Ludhiana	Cycle Parts – Handle, Chain, Pedal, Hub etc.	48 crores approx.
Unit – II (Head Office)	Ludhiana	Bicycles & Cycle parts – Fork, Frame, Chain cover	186 Crores approx.
Unit – III	Ludhiana	Steel pipes	–
Unit - IV	Ludhiana	Rim	6 Crores approx.

AVON group comprises of the following five companies:

	Group Companies	**Location**
1.	Avery Cycle Industries Limited	Ludhiana
2.	Avon Cycles Limited	Ludhiana
3.	Pahwa Cycles Private Limited	Ludhiana
4.	Pahwa Chains Private Limited	Chandigarh
5.	Avery Free Wheels Private Limited	Chandigarh

Products/Services

Cycles

Bicycle range has been classified into the following sections:

Roadster Bikes

There are 10 variants in this category including Royal Lady, Cheeta and Classic.

Mountain Bikes

These are wider tyre bikes suitable for mountain riding. Variations are; AVON Montage, AVON Oscar, AVON Teen Magic and AVON Carlos Elite.

City Bikes

Models of City Bikes are : AVON SLR Advantage, AVON Young Lady, AVON Challenger and AVON Rapid.

Kids Bikes

A big variety is available in Kids Bikes ; Giraffe, AVON Leo, AVON Bunny, AVON Superman, AVON Joey, to name a few.

Bicycle Parts and Accessories

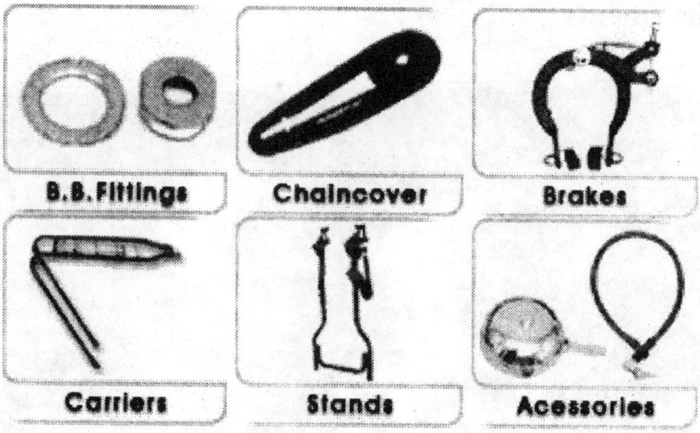

Awards and Certifications:

Avon has now obtained the Coveted ISO-9001 certification from TUV-Germany...

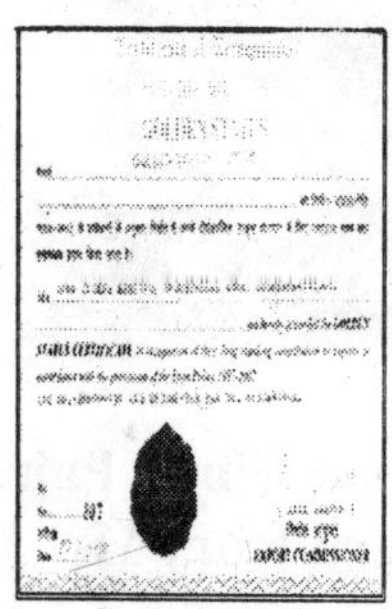

and Golden Trading House certificate from Ministry of Commerce, Govt. of India

Achievements

Onkar Singh Pahwa, CMD, AVON Cycles receiving award from Mr. Omar Abdullah

Onkar Singh Pahwa, CMD, AVON Cycles receiving award from Mr. Murosoli Maran, Hon'ble Industry Minister

Foreign Presence

AVON Cycles Limited is the largest manufacturer exporter of bicycles and bicycle parts from India. AVON goes to more than 80 countries worldwide. AVON Cycles Limited bagged the Top Exporter Award for fifth year running. To the overseas buyer, the company offers a choice of 50 plus models of bicycles and spares to suit a wide variety of market specifications. Quality at affordable price is made possible by a state-of-the-art manufacturing plant supported by most modern techniques and superior logistics. AVON is recognized by the Govt. of India as a 'Star Golden Trading House'.

Major export destinations include: UK, Africa, Germany, Switzerland, UAE, Egypt, Bangladesh and Nepal.

Competitors

The competitors of AVON cycles limited are:

1. Hero Cycles Limited
2. Atlas Cycles
3. TI Cycles

About Flagship Company

Avon cycles limited, located at G.T. Road, Ludhiana, is a major subsidiary of the group with an annual turnover of Rs. 300 crores. In spite of facing stiff competition from competitors like HERO, ATLAS and TI cycles, Avon has been able to expand its markets to almost whole of India while beyond the Indian shores it goes to more than 80 Countries world wide covering about 45% of the market in bicycles and bicycle parts. The company distinguished itself as the largest exporter for three years running thus establishing the brands ever growing popularity overseas.

Organisation Chart

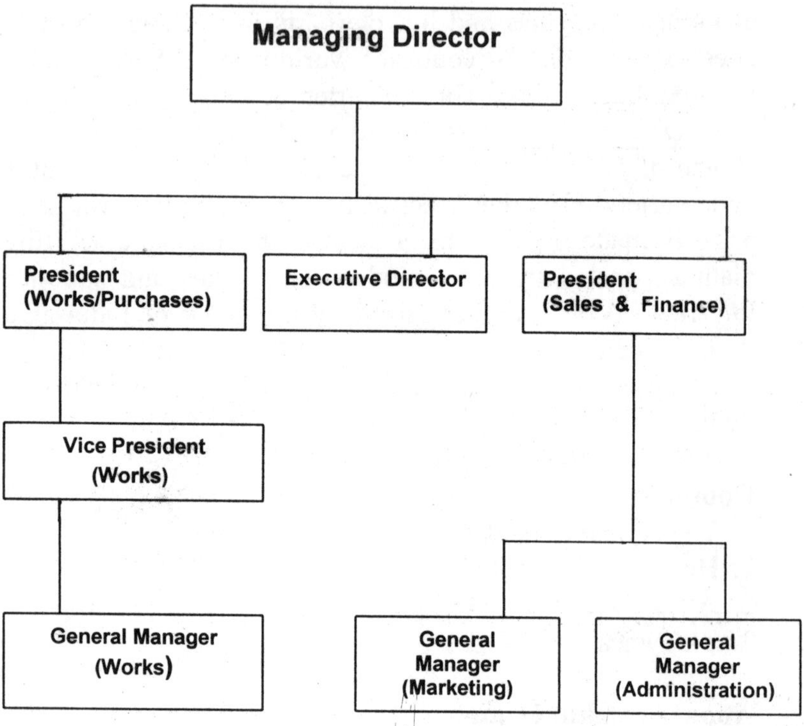

Avon is planning to undertake expansions and up gradation of existing facilities in the coming years with lot of new schemes in pipeline in the areas of infrastructure, new ventures, management and many more

Face to Face with Mr. P.K. Mahajan, General Manager (Marketing), AVON Cycles Limited

Mr. Mahajan attributed the success of Avon Cycles to its laborious and sincere employees who have strived hard and put in their best efforts to make Avon earn a name in the Cycle Industry.

He informed that Avon cycles have also put in a lot of emphasis on the development of its human resource. Workshops, Conferences, Executive and Workers development programmes are regular features in the organization. Proprietors of Avon Cycles consider their employees as a part of their family and HR policies of the organization give due concern to the employee welfare.

Mr. Mahajan admitted that Information Technology has contributed substantially to the changed face of the organization. Computers are being used in every department of the organization. Company has hired computer professionals and employees of the organization are also being trained to equip themselves with expertise in this field.

According to Mr. Mahajan the company is focusing on cost reduction measures to reduce the cost of production. Avon Cycles has also kept its profit margin quite low to have an edge over its competitors in the market. The same has resulted in products at cheaper rates leading to the increase in market share of the company. However, the company needs to focus on the development of in-house R&D facilities so that it can improve upon its products and incorporate new features.

When asked about future of Indian cycle industry in the light of low cost competition from China, Mr. Mahajan was fully confident that Indian cycle industry has enough capabilities to combat any threat from anywhere in the world. Industrialists of India are very enterprising and innovative and have the potential to excel in any kind of situation. Avon Cycles is proceeding with the immediate expansion and up gradation of the existing facilities.

Indians are capable enough to face challenges of

globalization. Government should contribute by more positive and long range policies.

Management Institutions have to play a major role and should try to put in practical exposure in their course curriculum so that budding managers can adjust in the fast paced industrial environment easily. Special emphasis should be placed on development of personality, team spirit, communication skills and business ethics.

Revealing initiatives taken by Avon Cycles to fulfill its social responsibilities, Mr. Mahajan informed that the group is supporting two hospitals, one serves the industrial population, the other one is located in the rural neighborhood of Ludhiana at Humbran.

Mr. Mahajan feels that Avon Cycles, in the hands of its young and dynamic leadership, is well on the fast track to become the leading player in the cycle industry of India.

Data Sheet

Year of Start	1952
Main Products/Operations	Bicycle & Bicycle Parts
Total Turnover	Rs. 600 crores
Domestic Turnover	60%
Foreign Turnover	40%
Certifications	ISO 9001 from TUV-Germany
Stock Exchange Listings	NIL
New Ventures	Upgradation & Expansion existing manufacturing facilities
Major Collaborations	Nil
Flagship Company	Avon Cycles Limited
Domestic Market	All over India
Foreign Markets	U.K., Africa, Germany, Switzerland, UAE, Egypt, Bangladesh, Nepal

3

Bhogal Group of Companies

Background and Historical Perspective

The Bhogal group was started by Sardar Karam Singh Bhogal in 1939 as a small manufacturing company dealing in bicycle components. It is counted among the first Indian companies who ventured into manufacture of bicycle components. This is one of those conglomerates, which can boast of being totally Indianised or indigenised company and has survived very well in the face of stiff competition.

This has been possible through maintaining strict Quality standards, cutting edge technology and cutting cost efficiently. But as said "Rome was not built in a day", this formidable giant started off as Chakkar & Company by two partners namely Sardar Karam Singh and Sardar Channan Singh. The company initially produced cycle parts like Hub cone, BBAxle and auto parts. This company started off with 6-10 employees. The initial employees were none other than youth who were formally thinking of entering military as soldiers. Thus the company was also one of the companies who gave the right direction to jobless yet efficient youth.

S. Mohinder Singh Bhogal s/o S. Karam Singh Bhogal separated from the parent company and launched a new company – Bhogals Sons – in April, 1948. Bhogal Sons, and Bhogal Exports, the exporting arm of the group, together consist of 5 companies spread over 25,000 Sq.Mtr. of area and employ more than 600 people.

Incorporation and Integration

Bhogal Group is a group of companies engaged in the manufacture of engineering goods and Software

Development. Established in 1939, Bhogal Sons (Regd.) was amongst the pioneers in India to manufacture Bicycle components. Today BHOGAL is a known brand in National as well as International markets. Bhogal is exporting to Europe, USA and other countries since 1960.

The software division was started in 1990. It started by providing customised software solutions to the manufacturing industry of Punjab as well as to its own group. Over the years Bhogal has acquired sufficient experience in analyzing customer's requirements, designing applications and successfully implementing them.

With expertise in Web Applications, Software Development and Back Office Applications, Bhogal has ventured into software export and providing IT enabled services.

Today, Bhogal is spread over 25,000 sq. meters of area and employs more than 600 people, with its turnover touching US $10 million. Bhogal Exports, which is an Exports House recognized by the Govt. of India, is accredited with ISO 9002 by the prestigious DNV of Holland.

Mission of Bhogal Group

- Bhogals will continue to evolve its resources, both intellectual as well as infrastructural, to cater to the requirements of customers. It will also strive to provide solutions which are simple, usable and functionally superior.
- To evolve our resources, both intellectual as well as infrastructural, to cater to the requirements of our customers by providing them high quality products and prompt services.

Awards/Certifications

The individuals and organizations striving to attain a high level of excellence in any field get recognition they deserve at hands of society and government. The Government too has ornamented Bhogals Group with many jewels. The story of progress, which Mohinder Singh made as the guiding spirit of the Bhogals, starting from scratch to the establishment of Bhogal Sons and its sister concern, is in fact the story of industrial revolution of the Punjab. Mohinder Singh and Bhogal Sons have been getting and still hold many honours and offices in local, state level and international organizations.

1. Best Industrial Unit in the State (1965-66) (Before the Division of Punjab)

2. Shield by Director of Industries, Punjab (1966)

This award was given for manufacturing Bicycles, Sewing machines and Quality components. They had 100% indigenous self designed machines.

3. Export Special Award (1980-81) (For Producing New Product BBAxle)

4. A.R. Bhatt Entrepreneurship Award (1984)

5. District Level Productivity Award (1985)

6. National Award for "Best Lab for Quality Product"(1995).

7. ISO-9002 Accredition by DNV for Bhogal Exports

Face to Face with Mr. M.S. Bhogal, Chairman and Managing Director

Bhogals started off under the flagship of Sardar Karam Singh Bhogal. The main aim of the organization was to stop foreign goods from taking the marketshare. Charan Singh was the partner in the partnership firm named Chakkar and Company. The initial product mix launched in the market was BBAxle48, Hubcone , Paddle Axle. Hub Cub was started in 1948.The partnership firm Chakkar and Company was located near Rekhi Cinema. The employees were the ones who were initially going to be recruited in army. Sardar Karam Singh imparted free service and free know how to them so that they could work in the firm. Their main strategy was to get local workers at less wages. This seemingly small firm grew to become a conglomerate. Currently they have 4 factories and one Exporting unit. Bhogal Exports, their exporting branch exports to European countries .

The group is focused to improve the quality of goods and earn a good name for the country. Their total turnover from domestic and foreign sales at present is Rs. 50-60 crores. Exports constitute Rs. 30 crore of the total turnover. Out of this, Rs. 20-22 crore is received from export of cycle parts.

Their Product Portfolio has increased considerably .At present their Product-Mix comprises of BBAxle, BB cup, Hub parts, Hub, Paddle, Free Wheel (on contract), Steel Bar (Product quantity of o/s not more than 100 P.C packet sealed). All products are carefully sealed, thus the chances of product getting lost by theft are nil. The Bhogals have currently launched SCOOZEE, a cycle for teenagers. Of late, Bhogal has ventured into IT Industry by offering IT Products such as Application Softwares & Web based solutions and services such as Back Office Operations.

Considering the current competitive trend the group is increasing its product portfolio.

Regarding the competitors, they believe that there is no direct competition so long as their products are of high quality .This they ensure by Stringent Quality tests in Lab and high Pricing by having uniform pricing policy. They ensure that the prices of their product remain the same through out the country by way of their chain of stockists.

The company believes in Quality. Bhogals have been awarded ISO9002 certification by the International Standards Organisation.

Thus the Quality Policy has been implemented throughout the organisation. The company believes in Customer care. If any Product is defective, it is immediately sent back to the company. This speaks a lot about their company which values Customer & its relationship with the company. Their products are used throughout India. But in terms of Quantity their main market is Uttar Pradesh.

In terms of the foreign market, they conform to the European market requirements. Bhogals attribute the success of their business to Quality and regular hard work. Mohinder Singh has a firm belief in the maintenance of quality of his goods He often says "Do not let the quality of goods to deteriorate, otherwise you would not survive." This adage has led to the development of 3 more sister concerns such as Bhogal Sales corporation, Bhogals Exports and Bhogals Private limited.

In the light of liberal imports from China, Bhogals are of view that there is absolutely no problem from China. Since in India the raw material is cheap as compared to the cost of raw material in China. A possible loophole that is working in favour of China is that Chinese Labour laws are not stringent. Their labour law consists of just 9 pages.

Labour has to work in 2 shifts of 10 hours each . Working hours are flexible in terms that working time can be increased from 10 to12 hours No extra payment is made for extra hours put in. There is no holiday or Sunday in China.. In India the labour scenario is not very bright since here labour work for 8 hours in 3 shifts.

They believe that the youth should be given Technical qualification amalgamated with Management education, as they consider that only such persons will be able to get work done in this Liberalisation, Privatisation, Globalisation (LPG) regime.

Wheel Pulley Mbk	**WPMBK 1**	**Wheel Pulley Mbk**	**WPMBK 2**
With Sprockets, Bearing & White Rings		With Sprockets, Bearing & Click Lever	
Teeth **Finish**	11, 12, 13. Black	**Teeth** **Finish**	11, 12, 13 Grey

Wheel Pulley Pgt		**Wheel Pulley Plastic**	
WHPGT 3 With Sprockets, Bearing & Click Lever		**WHPL 4** With Sprockets & Bearings.	
Teeth **Finish**	11, 12, 13. Grey	**Teeth** **Finish**	11, 12, 13. Black

The Complete Range of Bicycle Parts
Cotterless Bottom Bracket Axle
Bottom Bracket Axle
Bottom Bracket Bearing Cups
Bottom Bracket Bearing Cups with Ball Retainer
Front and Rear Hubs with Quick Release
Hub Axles with Quick Release
Chains
Chain Tensioners
Chain Wheels (Single and Multiple Speed)
Free Wheels (Single and Multiple Speed)
Hub Cones

About the Promoters

S.S. Bhogal: A Law graduate from Punjab University, has undergone EDP at IIM Ahmedabad and Bangalore. He has over 30 years experience in marketing in domestic as well as international markets. He is a widely travelled person and heads the Exports Unit of the group.

R.S. Bhogal: An engineering graduate with a diploma in Computer Applications, he is a hard-core Analyst Programmer with over 15 years of experience.

He has been responsible for total computerization of the Bhogal Group and has also developed process control software for in-house usage.

Kuljeet Singh: Graduated from Utkal university,

Bhubaneshwar, Orissa. He started his career as a Banker with Punjab & Sind Bank in 1980 and after working for 3 years, left banking to make a career in Computers. Since then he has worked in various capacities with Morgan Data Consultants, New Delhi, Kular Cycle Industries - Programmer, Case Computers - Branch Incharge, Viva Information Processing Pvt. Ltd. - Executive Director, Bhogal Management Services Pvt. Ltd. - General Manager, all at Ludhiana. He has tremendous experience in analyzing customer needs and designing efficient systems. At BE-IT he is heading the software development team.

Vishal Arora: An MBA from Pune University with a diploma in Web Applications. An upcoming computer wizard. He is part of the core group for web designing.

Offices

Head Office	732, Industrial Area-B, Ludhiana-141 003
Warehouse	G.T. Road, Dhandari Kalan, Ludhiana
Corporate Office	22-23 R, Industrial Area-B, Ludhiana
Overseas Office	13861 Harbor Boulevard, Garden Groove, CA 92843, USA, Tel: +1-714-554-2900 Fax: +1-714-554-2600

Data Sheet

Year of Start	1939
Main Products / Operations	Axels, Hubs
Total Turnover	Rs. 50-60 crores
Domestic Turnover	50%
Foreign Turnover	50%
Certificates	ISO 9002
Stock Exchange Listings	Nil
New Ventures	Software Development
Major Collaborations	Nil
Flagship Company	Bhogal Exports
Main Markets Being Served Domestic	All over India
Foreign	Europe

4

Eastman Industries Limited

Introduction: Bicycle and Bicycle Parts

Some Facts about the Bicycle Industry

1. Between January and April 2000 – 2,700,000 bicycles were produced in India and only 10,000 were imported.
2. During 1998 – 1999 the export of bicycles and parts was worth Rs.60 million.
3. During 1999 – 2000 the export of bicycles and parts increased to Rs.70 million.
4. In the years to come, the cycle industry is expecting to see significant growth.

Bicycle has been in use in India since 1890. Domestic demand of bicycles and bicycle parts used to be met by imports from UK, Japan and West Germany. In 1910, two SSI units came into existence at Calcutta for the manufacture of bicycle components and accessories. As the demand for bicycle parts, components and accessories increased, a number of SSI units came in up West and East Punjab, especially at Ludhiana and Malerkotla, in 1930. The first indigenously owned bicycle manufacturing unit, Atlas Cycles, was established at Sonipat in 1951 in the SSI sector in the undivided Punjab. Hero Cycles Limited commenced production of complete bicycles in 1956 as a SSI unit, and became the World's largest producer of Bicycles in 1987 by recording a production of 2,494,649 units and entered the Guinness book of World Records. They produced 5.5 million cycles during the year 2000. Though the Bicycle industry in India originated in Calcutta, Punjab became a fertile ground for its evolution and development. In the year 1960, around 400 units were reported in the small scale sector manufacturing bicycle parts and components in Punjab.

Due to reservation of almost all bicycle parts and components for exclusive manufacture in the small scale sector, this sector registered substantial growth in terms of both number of units as well as production. In fact, it has become the backbone of the complete bicycle industry.

Eastman entered the market with the manufacture of brakes for cycles in 1971. The Ludhiana cluster is producing about 60% of the bicycles produced in the country in the large and small scale sector, and more than 80% of the parts and components in large, medium, small and tiny sector. The main objective of EASTMAN is to produce quality products for the global market.

Hand Tool Industry: An Overview

Modernisation of small scale industry, specially hand tool industry in the small sector, has been recommended strongly because of the increasing gap between what is produced and what is required in the market. The industry has sustained itself so far because it was operating in sellers' market. The markets, however, were basically local. Vicissitudes of trade did not permit them to expand. However, with recent exposure to the international markets, the present products and operations reveal vast gaps that needed to be bridged urgently to register India's presence amongst the community of hand tool makers in the world. Bright future will belong to this industry in case it is able to play its role properly both in the local and international market.

Progress and prosperity of a society is the function of successful application of engineering techniques and scientific principles of management. Industry supplies needed goods and services to the society. Industrial progress means more goods, of better quality, to more and more people, at lesser cost. The industrial progress, interestingly, precludes hand tool development. Hand tool evolution and growth have waited for demand pressures to build up. Wilkinson's boring tool was built at the request of James Watt, who wanted his steam engines to perform better with properly finished bores. As the demand for accurate components has grown, precision standards of hand tools have also become more and more stringent.

Hand tools offered by small-scale sector fetch very low prices, which are the lowest in the world. Hand tools of low price category are not, however, made with cost reducing techniques except that they are produced by cheap labour. Small scale industry by itself will not be able to pull itself out from the present morass, without extraneous support. This is where Government assistance would be most welcome.

Eastman started manufacturing hand tools in 1992 through Eastman Cast and Forge Limited, Ludhiana and more than 80% of its products are being exported to major countries across the globe.

The Eastman Industries Ltd.: Profile

Background and Historical Perspective

Eastman Group was established in 1971 by Mr. J. R. Singal with an initial investment of Rs 25000 and 6 employees. Initial product was rubber for bicycle brakes. The first division, Eastman Rubber Industries was setup at 437-Industrial Area 'B' Ludhiana. The turnover of the company in the first year was Rs. 1,42,000/-.

The present business portfolio of Eastman consists of merchandising of bicycles, components and accessories as well as manufacturing of hand tools. The total turnover is

US $ 28 million out of which $ 1.8 million is from domestic business and the rest is from exports. Bicycle parts constitute $ 24 million and rest adds up to $ 4 million. Eastman hand tools and bicycles was started with $ 1million and the level of investment now is Rs. 30 crores. Its main competitors are Hero, Avon, Atlas and TL cycles.

The company is serving major OEMs in the domestic market. As far as exports are concerned, the main markets are Europe and Latin America. It is an ISO 9002: 1998 certified company and is planning to obtain ISO: 9001. It has a market share of 9%.

Family Hierarchy

J. R. Singal
(Managing Director, Eastman Industries Ltd.)

Shekhar Singal | Mrs. Darshana Singal **(Director)**

Mr. J. R. Singal, born on Jan 3, 1946, 55 years old, is a graduate having 28 years of experience in Small Scale Industry and Exports. The thrust area is Latin American countries. He is working as the Managing Director of Eastman Industries Ltd and Eastman Cast and Forge Ltd.

Mr. J. R. Singal has also held important positions in industry:

- Vice Chairman, Punjab State Council – CII
- Chairman, Bicycle Parts & accessories of EEPC
- Member – Punjab Export Promotion Board
- Member-Advisory Committee, Christian Medical

College and Hospital, Ludhiana

- Treasurer-Shree Guru Nanak Dev committee with Deputy Commissioner of Ludhiana as President, and Sh. S.P. Oswal as Vice President
- Member-Regional Advisory Committee of Custom Commisionrate, Amritsar

His wife Mrs. Darshana Singhal, 50, is a graduate and working as a Director. His son, Mr. Shekhar Singhal, 25, is a commerce graduate and an MBA from IMT, Ghaziabad.

Incorporation and Integration

Eastman Industries Limited was incorporated in the year 1982 by Mr. J. R. Singal. Ever since its establishment, the company has moved itself to the position of an ISO 9002 company, certified by KPMG world-wide quality registrars. The simple entrepreneurial philosophies and integrated corporate policies of Eastman Industries Limited have mobilised the company to become a Government approved Trading House, entirely focusing on international trade.

EIL is a fast mover on the global scene, supplying the world with quality bikes, components and accessories. A 100% export company, EIL is located in Ludhiana, the city that sets its pace by turning out a-bicycle-a-minute. Eastman is responsive to market trends, and serves business partners well with new product lines and healthy pricing.

Eastman industries limited has been a pioneer in exports to Middle East, Europe and Latin America. It took two decades of rigorous efforts, besides keeping itself abreast with latest innovations world over, to make it a leading name.

Drawing strength from the vast professional experience of its managers in this field, Eastman offers a myriad range of products to meet the stringent needs of the consumer.

Besides this it is recognised for its competitiveness in both quality and prices resulting in it being the most sought after single source vendor in the OEM and the replacement market.

With customer satisfaction as the central objective, Eastman has learned to adapt and grow to meet the changing requirements of its customers, to give them the ultimate advantage **"value for money".**

Mission Statement of Eastman Industries Limited

To make Eastman a preferred source of supply

- by providing the most appropriate products and services
- of the best possible quality
- in the fastest possible manner
- at the most reasonable prices.

Years to Remember for Eastman

1978: The first shipment of Eastman Group bicycle brake shoes leaves for foreign shores.

1980: Argentina bikes move on the road equipped with Eastman bike parts.

1980-1986: Good business ties develop with a few other Latin American countries.

1986 onwards: On to Europe, Middle East, Far East...

1986: Product adaptation and market research is initiated under World Bank project.

1997-1998: Eastman receives National Export Award from the Prime Minister of India.

2000: Quality above all! Eastman earns ISO 9002 accreditation.

2001: Quality in service! Web based dynamic product catalog and customer servicing features introduced.

Quality Policy

To ensure that the customer considers Eastman Industries Ltd. to be the primary source for his requirements.

Objectives

- To achieve Leadership in export markets.
- To search for new markets.
- To regain lost customers.
- To develop and export in case of established product category.

Strategy

- Continuous improvement in Quality System and quick redressal of customer complaints.
- Uniformity in specifications, OEM focused business presence in commercial fields, and timely delivery to customers.
- To improve capabilities by regular training of workers.
- Self answerability of employccs for effective communication.
- To assist vendors in product development and inform them regularly.
- To leverage Government policies for becoming better player.
- Flawless Auditing.

Products/Services

Eastman Industries Limited is manufacturer & exporter of a diversified range of bicycles, components and accessories, suitable for both conventional & contemporary bicycles. The company delivers complete bicycles, single speed and multispeed chain wheels, free wheels, axels, hubs, pedals, chains, frames, and other parts & accessories.

S. No.	Product	Brand	Year of Launch	Division
1	Rubber Spare Parts (Bicycle)	Eastman	1971	Industrial Area, Ludhiana
2	Bicycle Parts	Eastman	1975	Focal Point, Ludhiana
3	Hand Tools	Eastman	1992	G. T. Road, Ludhiana

Foreign Presence

The company has established its own brand 'Eastman' in Latin American countries including Panama. Eastman maintains pace with the technological developments, changing consumer behaviour and marketing and distributing strategies, to remain a competitive brand in the international market.

As a result of its excellent quality, time management, and price actualisation, Eastman has become a natural preference in the territories of Latin America, Europe (encircled Mediterranean region), and Middle East. The company foresees to deliver the same or better product quality, in a much wider market.

Trading House (Exports)

Eastman Industries Limited has been recognised as Trading House (Exports) by Ministry of Commerce,

Government of India, as per para 12.5 of EXIM policy of Government of India. FOB value of US$ 24 million in preceding financial year is required to become a Trading House (Exports).

The Group: Eastman Caste & Forge Limited

ECFL was incorporated in the year 1986, to manufacture hand tools and forging. The company, besides exporting to France, Belgium, Panama, Peru, Portugal, also sells through Export houses to Japan, Germany, Switzerland, Holland, and OEM's such as Hero Honda, TAFE, Swaraj, HMT, Kirloskar, Bajaj Auto, Mahindra & Mahindra.

The company has a manufacturing facility in a sprawling 70,000 square feet covered area at Ludhiana. The ECFL plant manufactures a wide range of carbon steel and chrome vanadium Hand – Tools.

With ISO 9002 certified facility for manufacturing, ECFL started with an edge when it bagged prized O.E. accounts like Mahindra & Mahindra, Bajaj Auto – World's largest manufacture of scooters having collaboration with Kawasaki of Japan for motorcycles, Hero Honda limited, new Holland tractors – (India) a unit of world known Ford Tractors, HMT, Tafe, Swaraj Tractors and others. In a nutshell ECFL is fully equipped to satisfy all kinds of customers.

Besides OE suppliers, Eastman tools are widely accepted across the nation and in international markets. The company takes pride in declaring that it has also earned **German product safety standard** certification by TUV Rheinland another step forward on its path of continual advancement towards total customer satisfaction.

A great deal of customization, tailored packaging and professional services place Eastman in a selected brand of vendors for a host of buyers across the globe.

CICLOMETA, an international concern of repute took up the assignment of distributorship for Eastman Industries Ltd. in the year 1989. Ever since its association with Eastman, Ciclometa displayed earnest devotion and worked skilfully for the distribution of Eastman bike parts in Mexico. The products, Bikes, Bike parts & accessories from Eastman, have gained the status of most preferred goods in the Mexican market.

Ciclometa takes every initiative to promote the goods from Eastman by continuously participating in trade fairs held in Mexico. While participating in promotional activities, their sole concern remains to propagate the name of Eastman among serious customers of Mexican bike industry.

Eastman takes pride in saying that due to this collaboration, the Eastman brand has become the most preferred brand for bike parts in Mexico. The Eastman family appreciates and congratulates Ciclometa for its valuable contribution and believes that this relation of reliability and goodwill will continue forever.

Diversification and Expansion

- Eastman Industries Ltd. has installed state-of-the-art CNC machine to manufacture all kinds of plastic moulded parts for bicycles, mopeds and motorcycles.
- Eastman will have future ventures in production, state-of-the-art bicycle components and accessories. They are likely to have future ventures in Latin America as it is a thrust area identified by them.

ORGANIZATION CHART

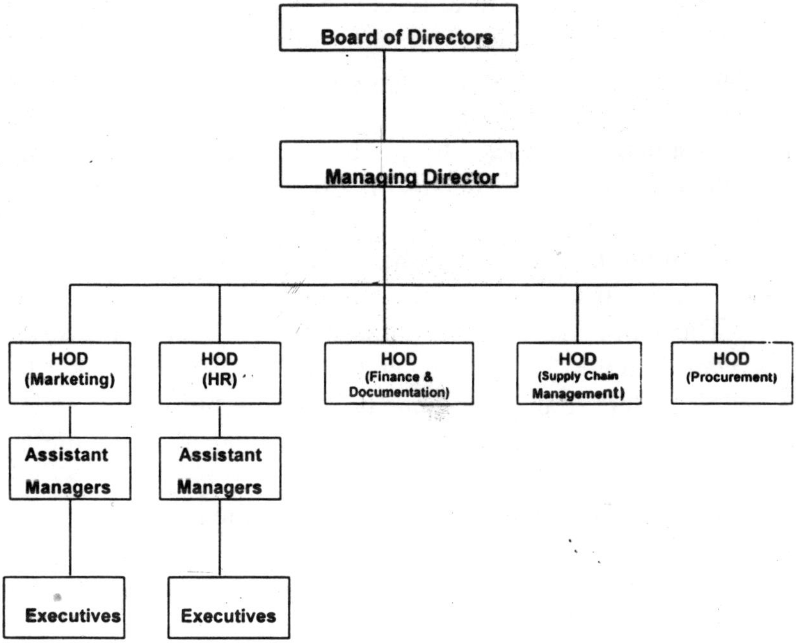

Awards and Certifications

Eastman Industries Ltd was incorporated in the year 1982 with Sh. J. L. Singal as Promoter. The company has moved itself to the position of a company with ISO 9002 certification by KPMG world-wide quality registrars. The company is manufacturer & exporter of a diversified range of components and accessories for bicycles with established brand name "*Eastman*" in Latin America and selected European countries.

Eastman Industries Ltd has been recognised as Trading House (Exports) by Ministry of Commerce, Government of India, as per para 12.5 of EXIM policy. FOB value of US$ 24 million in preceding financial year is required to be recognised as a Trading House (Exports)

The company was honoured with the National Export Award Trophy for the financial year 1997-98 presented by Hon'ble Shri Atal Bihari Vajpayee, Prime Minister of India. Only 20 companies in India are honoured at the National Level each year.

In 1999-2000 Eastman Industries Limited received ITPO UAC Focus Award.

The company also earned *"German product safety standard"* certification by TUV Rheinland.

Strength of Eastman

- Eastman is comfortable doing business with Latin American countries. Arabs, Europeans and now China are going to join the list of global business partners this year.
- The team members of Eastman study the markets well and keep in touch with latest developments in the area of operation.
- Eastman team is quick to help clients on critical issues:

- ❖ What to stock?
- ❖ When to stock?
- ❖ How much to stock?
- India is one of the largest bicycle markets in the world, and Eastman exclusively focuses on global business. Its business practices and product developments reflect world-wide trends and this makes Eastman easy to work with.
- The packaging has been standardised after a careful study of requirements of different types of customers.
- Eastman has intense and external testing facilities to ensure all aspects of quality like:
- ❖ Physical/chemical properties of raw materials
- ❖ Process control
- ❖ Dimensional integrity
- ❖ Finishing
- ❖ Packing
- Strict control is exercised on the manufacturing process. First grade materials are used. Periodic evaluation is done of materials and processes.
- Quality control assurance department monitors the product and carries out regular inspections.
- When an order is negotiated, the standards of quality are never compromised to accommodate a price.
- Quality norms must endure, even if it means squeezing earnings. A relationship built in quality has a solid foundation, and a satisfied customer is more important than quick short-sighted gain.

Face to Face with Mr. J.R. Singhal
Chairman-cum-Managing Director

- Mr. Singhal attributed the success of EIL to his wife and parents.

- Mr. Singhal views that the criticality of HRM is touching the heart of employees as HRM is the main area of success of business and in merchandising trade product is people, market is people and service is people.
- According to Mr. Singhal, Ludhiana will not be able to have a phenomenon growth until we all in the Ludhiana industry mature ourselves and realise the grand base. When the competition sets in and each fiscal in the times to come will look to be a better year than present one. Now the emergence of Chinese good will lead some fair persons to probably go out of business and new generation will come in the business and whatever will be produced in Ludhiana will be out priced internationally. Chinese goods are going to find grip in Indian market because duties are going to go down further.
- Mr. Singhal views Indian firms have started a thinking process in Ludhiana only to remain competitive and they are going to face this challenge and have started afloat in the long run. The SSI sector will suffer the most because till now they have not realised the fact of SSI.
- Talking about globalisation, Mr. Singhal states that Eastman is concentrating on Marketing Research and research in all aspects of business:
- ❖ Redefining the business processes.
- ❖ Cost cutting in operations.
- ❖ Training employees on regular basis whether inside or outside.
- ❖ Sharp focus on each activity.
- It has benefited Eastman reasonably well particularly in research aspects.

Main Strengths

- Experience in international trade.
- Causing commitment to customers/employers to the supplies of good and services.

Main Weakness

- Expectations from the people working for the company are higher than the grand reality in Ludhiana.
- Delegation is more than expected at many occasions where a person will pull out.
- We are fair but not firm in dealing the situations where people ditch us.
- Because of a firm mind on dispatching of quality goods, we visibly loose money, which gets paid up after a long term.
- Mr. Singhal holds the view that the management education needs up gradation according to industry requirements and quality stuff is required.
- Visualising the group after 10 years, Mr. Singhal said, “the group will have a phenomenal growth because Eastman is in tune with the global competition and trying to develop HR, which is to do a business today”.

Data Sheet: Eastman Industries Limited*

Year of Start	1982
Main Products/Operations	Manufacturer & Exports of Bicycle parts & Accessories
Total Turnover	Rs. 45 crores
Domestic Turnover	Rs. 1 crore
Foreign Turnover	Rs 44 crores
Compound Annual Growth Rate Of Sales For Last 10 Years	10-20%
Certificates	ISO: 9002, SGS Gold Seal
Stock Exchange Listings	No
New Ventures	No
Major Collaborations	No
Main Markets Being Served Domestic	NIL
Foreign	Latin American Countries

*This sheet belongs to Eastman Industries only (Not for entire group)

Key Persons

M.D.

J. R. Singal

Director

Darshana Singal

Marketing Head

Satyam Wadhwa

HR

D.S. Sandhu

Finance & Documentation Head

Sushil Sachdeva

Procurement Head

Kultar Singh

Accounts Head

Lakhwinder Singh

IT Head

Vijay Sharma, Jaspal Singh

Production Head

Narinder Mohan, Vipin Gupta

5

F M I Limited

Introduction

Ludhiana is commonly known as the Manchester of India and also as the Industrial Capital of Small Scale Industry in the country. The origin of the town can be traced to the year 1481 A.D. when the Lodhi established fort here. There was hardly any industry worth the name in the year 1947 in Ludhiana. The Muslims who constituted the major working force in the industry, migrated to West Pakistan leaving a great gap to be filled up. The refugees who came from west Pakistan after partition and settled at Ludhiana, were very enterprising and hard working people. They immediately took up the industry ventures for their livelihood and this was the start of industrial development of the city. Mr. Madan Nayar, Chairman cum Managing Director and founder of the group, took the initiative and proposed the installation of a plant for manufacture of measuring tapes. At that time Ludhiana was a growing city and Government of India was providing sufficient aid to the entrepreneurs.

Ludhiana has seen enormous industrial growth during the last 4/5 years due to significant improvement in the law and order situation. A conducive atmosphere for the growth of industry is apparent. Lot of investment is coming in industrial ventures from within Punjab and from outside Punjab. A large number of units have come up both in small scale as well as in large & medium scale sectors. A variety of items such as cycle and cycle parts, sewing machines and components, automobiles parts and accessories, hosiery and knitwear goods, industrial fasteners, machine tools and components, rubber goods, woollen garments, electronic goods, etc. are being produced in the small scale sector. The industry in large and medium sectors is producing items like bicycles, hosiery goods, vanaspati, tyres, tubes, electronic goods, steel and alloy steel castings, beer, sugar, flour, rice bran oil, cattle feed, etc. Freemans enjoys a monopoly in the market and the company has no competitor in the region. The company has brought fame to the region by exporting its product to major markets in the world.

The Freemans: Profile

Background/Historical Perspective

FMI Ltd. was started in 1950 with an initial investment of about Rs. 10,000/-. This was the money which Mr. Madan Nayar, present Chairman and Managing Director of the company, received in aid from the Government of India after moving from Pakistan to India.

For the first time measuring tapes were manufactured in India, and marked the beginning of the measuring tools industry.

The first unit was started with 30 employees at Iqbal Ganj, Ludhiana. The organization today has an annual turnover of Rs.20 Crores.

Family Tree

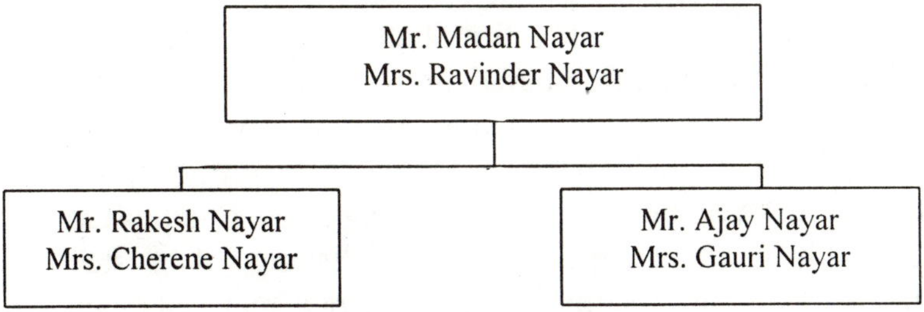

Incorporation and Integration

FMI Ltd. started manufacturing of metal wired measuring tapes in 1950. In 1965 it pioneered the manufacturing of Steel tape measures and Tape Rules in the country with American know how. To establish distribution network for serving European countries, EURO FREEMANS S.A. was established in 1988 in Barcelona (Spain). Presently FMI Ltd. is serving markets in over 60 countries around the world, which include European and American territories. This has resulted in an increased market penetration in Europe. FMI Ltd. is the pioneer and largest manufacturer of Tape Measures in the Indian Subcontinent.

Mission Statement of FMI Ltd.

"COMMITMENT TO PERFECTION THROUGH QUALITY AND CUSTOMER SATISFACTION "

Preamble

We, the management of Freeman (FMI Ltd.) here set forth our belief as to the purpose for which the company is established and the principles under which it should operate. We pledge our effort to the accomplishment of these purposes within these principles.

Market Orientation

Precision, quality, and a firm belief in perfection has resulted in continuous upgradation of technology and expansion of existing production facilities to meet the growing demand. Under backward integration, the group has installed steel treatment plants and slitting lines for tape steel strips with German know-how. Establishing of a steel division with better quality control over raw materials gave FMI an edge over competitors. It also has a plastic division with over 15 injection moulding machines for manufacturing plastic components. For this reason it is competitive in international markets as well.

Steel rule, spirit levels and hand tools added a new dimension to the activities of FMI. Of course the practice of stringent quality control is still in place and FMI is catering to the markets of over 62 countries around the world.

Awards/Certifications

Quality Standards and Approvals

Long Steel Tape	Fibre Glass Tape	Steel Tape Rules
EEC E92 00.014	EEC E92 00.006 E92 00.007	EEC E98 07.011 E98 07.006
Class-II	Class-III	Class-II

ISO 9002

FMI got EEC (European Economic Community) approval which is a testimony to the fact that their tape measures conform to the best international quality standards. FMI also has ISO 9002 quality certification.

To establish distribution network for serving the European Countries, **EUROFREEMANS** S.A. was established in Barcelona (Spain) which substantially increased the market penetration in Europe.

FMI Ltd. strives to meet customers aspirations, satisfaction and confidence in quality, reliability, aesthetics and economy through high innovation, creativity, Zero Defect approach by constant upgradation of quality and human excellence to stay in global main stream. FMI Ltd. designs its products in such a way that they have above average quality. When FMI Ltd. announces "New and Improved Products" it means it.

Foreign/Domestic Presence

In the 1970's, the Company started marketing its products in Spain, Peru and Chile, and shifted to USA market in late 80's. Presently, European market constitutes 50% of exports of Freemans Measures. The company has 82 distribution offices across the world.

As far as domestic market is concerned, main distribution offices are established in 4 metro towns of India, and more than 100 distributor-cum-dealers are appointed all over India. New Delhi is the main hub for distribution.

Future Plans

FMI Limited plans to strengthen its products through a process of value additions. It also proposes to strengthen its Research and Development effort through stronger in-house Research and Development. It may occasionally outsource limited R&D requirements.

Diversification/Product Portfolio

The main products of the company are measuring tapes of all types- metal Wired, glass fiber, & steel tapes, rules, scales, cutters and spirit levels. FMI Ltd. is also engaged in manufacturing and export of a variety of hand tools, which include pliers, hammers, spanners, pipe wrenches etc.

S. No.	Year of Start	Main Products/ Operations
1	1950	Metal Wired tapes
2	1966	Steel Tapes
3	1980	Fiber Glass Tapes
4	1988	Cutters
5	1997	Scales
6	1998	Spirit Level

Steel Tape Measures

Fibre Glass Tape Measures

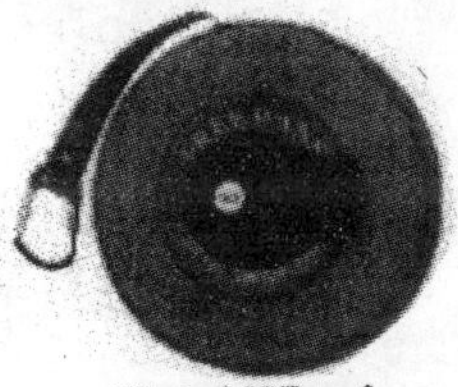

Metal Wired Tape Measures

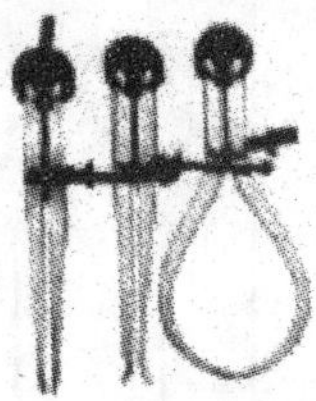

Spring Calipers

Steel Tape Rules

Cutters

Spirit Levels

Steel Rules

Organization Structure

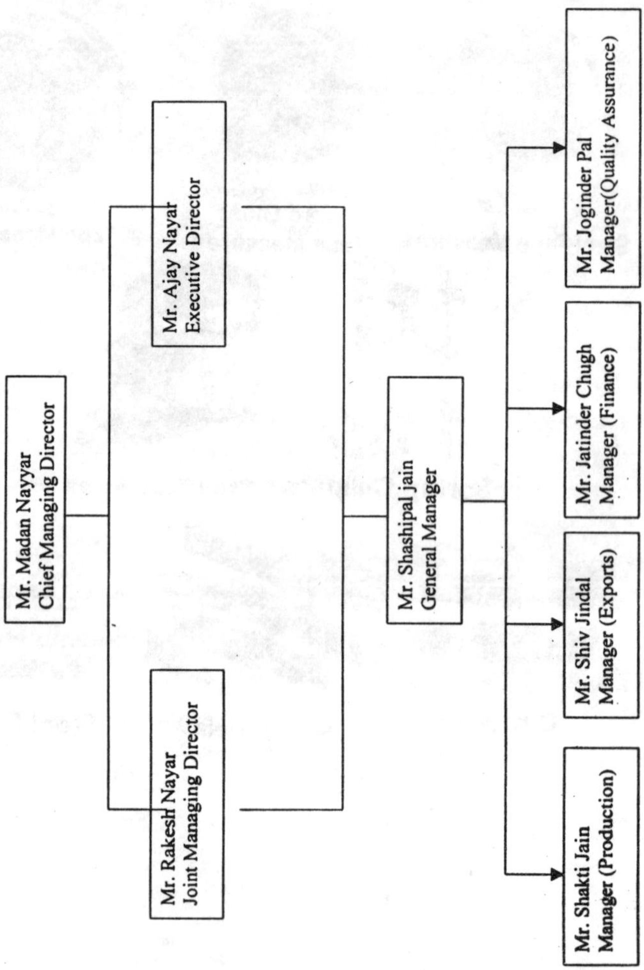

Face to Face with Mr. Ajay Nayar, Executive Director

During conversation, Mr. Ajay Nayar, Executive Director, FMI, touched upon various aspects of FMI Ltd. He attributed the success of the business to the foresight and hard work of Mr. Madan Nayar, who started the business with Rs. 10,000 immediately after partition. Mr. Madan Nayar is the brain behind the grand success FMI Ltd. has achieved today.

When asked about competitiveness of Indian firms to face challenges of globalization, he responded that Indian firms are not very competitive. Indian firms are weak on the cost front also because raw materials are costlier. The problem is multiplied by the low productivity of Indian labour. Ever-increasing taxes are further adding to the problems of Indian business. The position on labour front is very gloomy because India has not yet taken up labour reforms. He said that although wages of Chinese workers were same as that of Indian workers, Chinese labour was far more productive. Companies will have to go for cost reduction for tackling the global challenges even if the options are limited.

He stated that information technology benefits are real for business as information flow gets speeded up and economies of scale are realized. The organization is benefiting from new techniques like process re-engineering and Enterprise Resource Planning, which are making systems more effective.

When asked about the role of government in supporting business Mr. Nayar was not very happy. He said that although policies like soft rate of interest for credit, relaxation and exemption from labour loss, subsidized raw material and technological support provided by the government have helped the industry, Government had created more problems by shielding Indian Business from global competition for a long period of time. He said that incentives should be given as and when required, but continuous easy incentives tend to create inefficiency in the business firms.

Mr. Nayar opined that Human Resource is a very important part of any organization. The success of an organization depends on capability of its human resource. Human Resources are a source of balance, motivation and good discipline. In today's competitive era, it is the intellectual capital which acts as a competitive edge for an organization. When asked about educational institutes Mr. Nayar said that B-schools like IIMs provided very rich and practical-oriented education. The performance of students passing out from these institutions was very good. He believed that in order to bring regional institutes at par with industry requirements there should be more practical orientation in education. These regional institutes should increase their interaction with industry. It is only through real- life orientation of education that the students can mould their skills according to the requirements of industry.

Managers and technical graduates of today should be honest and should have integrity. The ability to adapt to the changing business environment must be present to enable them to face the challenges of business. The need of today is efficient and smart workers. These are yet not available in India. Mr. Nayar said that worker's participation in management is at times an eye-opener to the management. He added that after getting ISO 9002 certification management started encouraging departmental heads to contribute in the organizational meetings. The results obtained were much more than expected. Even the grass root workers started giving innovative ideas and suggestions when asked for.

When asked about the future of Ludhiana Industry in the light of emergence of competition from countries like China, Mr. Nayar replied that it was going to be a case of survival of the fittest. Only big companies with large resources and ability to control costs could face the threat from China. Large companies can achieve economies of scale and hire consultants to help improve upon their skills. Small companies with scarce resources were not in a position to take on of low prices competition. Further, the government had to take drastic steps to simplify its procedures.

Mr. Nayar emphasised the importance of specialisation for penetration into local and international markets. Talking about the future operational plans, he said that FMI Ltd. was planning to diversify within measurement related products only because other fields were already too crowded.

Data Sheet

Year of Start	1950
Main Products/ Operations	Measuring Tapes of all types – Metal Wired, Glass Fibre, Steel Tapes, Rules, Scales, Cutters and Level Vials.
Total Turnover	Rs. 2500 Lacs
Domestic Turnover	Rs. 1500 Lacs
Foreign Turnover	Rs. 1000 Lacs
Compound Annual Rate Growth Rate of Sales for Last Two Years	10%
Certification	ISO 9002 , EEC approval
Sock Exchange Listing	No
New Ventures	No
Major Collaboration	No
Flag Ship Company	No
Main Markets (Domestic)	All over India 4 Metros
Main Markets (Foreign)	Export 40% including Europe, USA (In all 62 countries around the world)
Competitors	Chinese Products

Names and Address of Key People

Regd. Office

Ferozepur road, Ludhiana-141001 India
Phone No.0161-402423/24/25,402440/41
Fax:- 0161-400793,402422
Website:-www.freemans - tapes.com

CMD

Mr. Madan Nayar

JMD

Mr. Rakesh Nayar

ED

Mr. Ajay Nayar

GM

Mr. Shashi Jain

Production Manager

Mr. Shakti Jain

Finance Manager

Mr. Jatinder Chugh

Quality Assurance Mgr.

Mr. Joginder Pal

Export Manager

Mr. Shiv Jindal

6

G.S. Auto International Limited

Introduction: Indian Auto Part Industry

Evolution of Indian Auto Part Industry

Although India was an early entrant in the automotive market, 1984 was a landmark year with Maruti Suzuki appearing on the scene with new models of cars. With it, came in new technology and bigger volumes. Yet, for about 15-16 years thereafter, there wasn't much headway as Maruti was only concentrating on the 800cc vehicle. Barring small volume production of Zen and the Esteem, there was not much dynamism in the automotive scenario that could egg on suppliers. Then, came the multinationals like General Motors, Ford, Fiat, Daewoo and others; some have had their vendors like Delphi and Visteon following them.

Now the challenge is to see how much share of the business they would take away from the Indian auto component market - remember that Delphi alone is a $36 billion company whereas the total auto component industry size in India is about $3 billion. So, we are not really talking about equals in any sense.

As the industry evolves, it is likely that the Tier I suppliers will be the Delphis and the Visteons who have worked with their own manufacturers in other countries as well. So, Indian auto component makers may eventually become Tier II and Tier III suppliers.

Comparison of Indian Auto Part Industry with Other Countries

The auto component industry which had its beginning in

Japan in the 1950s was protected for a good 40 years; however, it was nurtured by its mother industry which made great headway in technology and supplied vehicles for the global market. The Korean market even today doesn't have a very liberal policy that supports imports. There are non-tariff barriers that control free import of automotive components into Korea. In India, despite the fact that we were early entrants in the automotive industry, the vehicle industry, be it trucks or cars, did not constantly come out with any new models. As a result of this, the auto part makers had no challenge to upgrade technology.

Effects of Globalisation on Auto Part Industry

Definitely, companies like Hyundai and Ford, which have localized procurement of parts to a large extent, have helped Indian auto part industry to upgrade technology either internally or tie-up with their suppliers overseas. The only area of concern is the MNC auto companies commitment to localization. For instance, it is not sure whether Honda has policy for localization. If a component maker imports a sub-assembly and supplies it to India, it is localized from the vehicle manufacturers point of view. But truly speaking, the component itself is not localized; customers will be paying for spares in dollar terms.

Future of Auto Part Industry

The Indian industry has been asked to swim against the tide in a very short span of time. In India, the auto-policy changes from time to time. Further, the Indian component industry needs to improve in terms of reliability of supply, quality of supply and timeliness of supply. Toyota is able to get four supplies a day from vendors in Bangalore and daily supplies from rest of vendors in India This has to be the trend for Indian auto component industry to survive and we need to step up towards hourly supplies.

The ability to innovate will take a long time and this is why many Indian part makers will not make it to Tier I supplier position. In terms of cost, the vehicle manufacturers, world over except component manufacturers, to drop prices every year by two to three per cent and this is going to be a Herculean task bearing in mind inflation rate of around four per cent. This means that the labor productivity, space productivity, capital and raw material productivity will have to more than to offset the inflation rate so that the prices can be held for three to four years. Very few companies in India are in a position to compete in the world market. Heads of majority of the companies don't want to compete in the world market because of lot of hassles involved – a lot of upfront investment is needed to promote exports; about three to four per cent of sales on research and development and, one to two per cent in market promotion, travel and sales.

No doubt, getting on world map is need of the hour. If Indian companies don't do so they will not be able to build up volumes to compete with MNCs like Delphis and Visteons. Unfortunately, export has neither been the thrust nor the strength of the auto-component industry and they have to take a re-look at it.

Areas Where Indian Companies Can Compete Effectively in Global Markets

Indian component companies are competitive in the commodity range of products like fasteners, valves, brake linings, and some chassis parts.

Of course, companies might face the catch-22 situation while aspiring to become OE suppliers, as OE suppliers need support of warehousing for complying to the JIT demands of vehicle manufacturers. So, new aspirants to global markets could take the first step ahead by focusing on the after-markets.

The G.S. Group: Profile

Background/Historical Perspective

The genesis of the present GS Group dates back to 1938 when late Baba Gurmukh Singh Ji started manufacturing bicycle components. Baba Gurmukh Singh Ji was a self made person, devoid of parental love & education. He started working as an apprentice in a smithy shop in his native village near Machiwara at the age of 12 years.

Later on he started a venture of his own and soon started making automotive components of the improved vehicles. Flagship Company of the group GS Auto International was private Ltd. Company till 1985 and was known as GS and

Sons (P) Ltd. but was converted to public Ltd. Company afterwards.

Outsourcing is an inseparable activity when it comes to manufacturing automobiles. With reigning in of globalization the most affected part of business is sourcing along with marketing and finance. With endless list of international players in auto component manufacturing everyone in the fray is feeling the heat of competition and GS group is amongst those who are taking on to these tides bravely.

Presently group is endorsing its presence through a vast dealer network with more than 500 dealers mapping the whole nation, as well as making marks abroad via sales offices. Change is theme of life nowadays and GS follows the same. Group is continuously getting benefits by successfully employing management and quality techniques like 5S, JIT (just in time) aiming towards TPM/TQM.

Group is presently operating in OEM and replacement markets and is also growing overseas .The clients of the group who have shown faith in competitiveness of GS include Ashoka Leyland, Hindustan Motors, Delphi Automotive Systems, Swaraj Mazda, PTL, Maruti and VOLVO.

Flagship Company Profile

Company Name:	G.S.Auto International Limited
Board of Directors:	Giani Bhagat Singh, Chairman
	S. Jagat Singh, MD
	S. Jasbir Singh, ED
	S. Surinder Singh (Finance Director)
Bankers:	Bank of Baroda, Ludhiana

Punjab & Sind Bank, Ludhiana
Punjab National Bank, Ludhiana

Capital	
Issued:	Rs. 20 million
Paid Up:	Rs. 17 million
Line of Business:	Automobile Components
Links in Chain:	G.S.Auto International Limited G.S. Radiators Limited G.S. Sales Corporation Ryait Exports

Incorporation and Integration

The GS group has constituent companies namely GS Auto International Ltd., GS Radiators, GS Sales Corporation, Ryait Exports, GS Foods and GS Hydro Pneumatic (P) Ltd.

GS AUTO INTERNATIONAL LIMITED

GS Auto International Ltd. is the flagship company of the group. Started in 1938 today GS Auto International Ltd. has got a team of 1000 young dedicated technicians looking for excellence in quality and workmanship. Sound engineering skills of a dedicated workforce honed over a period of 50 years is the main weapon in the GS armoury. Cost effectiveness and customer service is at its best when coupled with latest state of art equipment supported by Computer Aided Design (CAD), Computer Aided Manufacturing (CAM) and Computer Aided Engineering.

Family Tree

Baba Gurmukh Singh ji
(1900-1979)
Founder

S. Bhagat Singh
(Elder Son)

S. Jagat Singh
(Younger Son)

Ranjodh Singh
(Ex. Director)
GS Radiators

Jasbir Singh Ryait
(Jt. Mg.Director-GS Auto)
International Ltd.)

Mr. Surinder Singh Ryait
(Director Commercial)

(CAE). Centre bolts, U-bolts, Hub bolt, King Pins, Computer Aided are passed through numerous steps at stages of design, raw material procurement process.

All the guidelines from quality manual are followed and GS Auto International is having quality certifications both in forms of ISO 9002 and QS 9000.ISO 9002 was obtained by the company in 1997–98 and QS 9000 in 2000 .QS-9000 is a Quality certification on the theme of ISO 9000 but with a difference.

GS Auto has joined a cluster of fourteen Indian companies in January 2001 under the program initiated jointly by ACT, ACMA Centre of Technology and CII (Confederation of Indian Industry). The mission of this program is to bring about improvement in the production processes by way of concept propagated and practised by major automotive companies the world over. Under the joint program the cluster member companies are required to carry out self-audition and improvements in house.

Awards and Certifications

GS AUTO is accredited with QS 9000 and ISO 9002 Certifications by BVQI, U.K. Each component passes through numerous tests at the stages of design, raw-material inspection & of course throughout the manufacturing process. Conformance to the quality begins at shop floor, with each worker following the quality guidelines as laid down in the Quality Manual. The Following quality system requirements are taken care of at GS Auto for conformance to quality standards, on-time delivery, maintaining product quality and handling customer's complaint.

1. APQP (Advanced Product Quality Planning)
2. PPAP (Production Part Approval Process)
3. FMEA (Failure Mode Effect Analysis)

4. SPC (Statistical Process Control)
5. MSA (Measurement System Analysis)

Also they are implementing and practicing 5-S, TPM, TQM and TPS concepts, with the involvement of all the workers and employees. QS9000 / ISO-9002 Certificates are the endorsements to their commitment to continuous improvements in quality.

Quality Policy

To achieve leadership in product quality and to have sustained growth through satisfaction of customer's needs.

Quality Objectives

- Strictly adhering to the documented systems, procedures, work instructions, and specifications at all stages.
- Development of employees at all levels of organisation through continuous training and education.
- Minimise wastage by doing the things right at the first time.
- Cost reduction in areas of operations to remain competitive.

GS Radiator's Limited

Started in 1992, GS Radiators is carrying out manufacturing operations by adopting the latest technology from Calsonic Llanellc Radiators Ltd, UK .It has developed a wide range of radiators for almost all vehicle manufacturers in India like: -Telco, Ashok Leyland, Swaraj, Mazda, Swaraj Tractors, Mahindra & Mahindra and

Hindutan Motors.

The plant is equipped with full fledged design facilities with expert design skills, calibration facilities, as well as tool room having latest machines with high level precision. Facilities are also available for prototype development and testing. Due to these R&D efforts GSR has developed and supplied Radiators for latest generation vehicles like VOLVO, Saab and Mazda 626.The total investment in GS radiator stands at Rs. 358 lac and total turnover of the firm is over Rs. 1608 Lacs.

GS Sales Corporation

The firm was started in 1994 to provide a platform to the local units by exploring synergies .The products under brand name "Jagat International include a range of truck & tractor parts. The components are being marketed throughout India.

Company's Name
G.S. Sales Corporation
Place of Business
G.S. Estate, Political. Box No. 712
G.T. Road, Ludhiana-141 003 (INDIA)
Year of Establishment
1994
Line of Business
Trading of Auto Parts & Hand Tools
Customers
Indian Replacement Market
Bankers
Canara Bank

Every Business has to survive with in the periphery of healthy and unhealthy environment. The mushrooming up of small manufacturing units in the last two decades and absence of any marketing support–system added to the plight of small manufacturers.

Products under the **JAGAT** brand name include wide range of truck, tractor parts, being marketed throughout India.

Ryait Exports

Ryait Export established in 1988, having Flagship G.S. Auto International Ltd. (Year of estab. 1938), which is one of the largest O.E. supplier to various Indian and International Automobile giants. Cottage Industry has been the backbone of the Indian economy. Major chunk of our Export basket include goods produced by skilled artisans in the remote villages. Promotion and recognition of their skill is our prime concern. Early 90's witnessed server forex crunch following which, Exports began to be perceived as patriotic activity, It apparently became imperative for the Indian manufacturers to go global. The company is engaged in Export of Handtools, Automotive components for commercial Vehicles, Machine tools and steel. Agricultural Implements and Handicrafts are other Items on the shelves.

Line of Business: Exports of Consumable Items, Engineering Goods, Agriculture Implements, Machine Tools and Handicrafts.

Products/Services

Name of the Company	Year of Start	Main Products/ Operations
G.S Auto International Ltd	1948	Automotive Components Cast: Shakle,Brackets,Plates,Clamps (2 Kg-20 Kg) Forged: Wheel/Hub bolts,Washers,High and Castle nuts(hot as well as cold) Machined: King pin kits,Spring Pins,Axle Studs,CheckNuts,Bushes,U-bolts,Centre bolts
G.S.Radiators Ltd.	1992	Radiators for all Automobiles mainly Telco. Ashok Leyland, Swaraj,Hindustan Motors, M&M and European Models
G.S. Sales Corporation	1994	Marketing of Truck and Tractors parts under brand name GSC throughout India outsourcing from domestic manufacturers
Ryait Exports	1988	Exports of Hand Tools,Automotive components,Machine Tools& Steels,Handicraft & Agricultural implements.

Organisation Chart

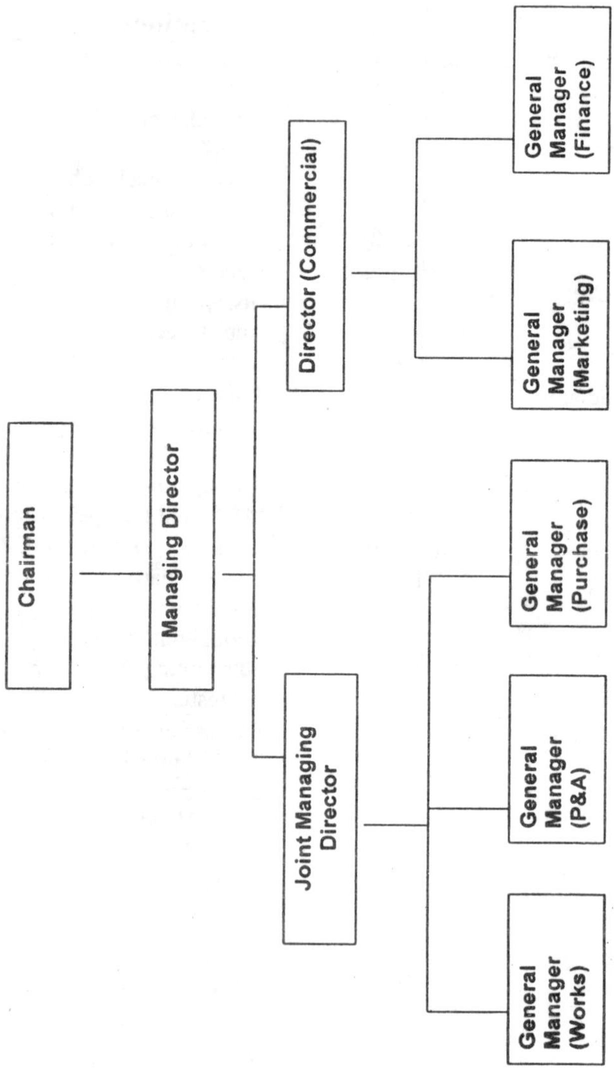

Main Products of GS Auto International

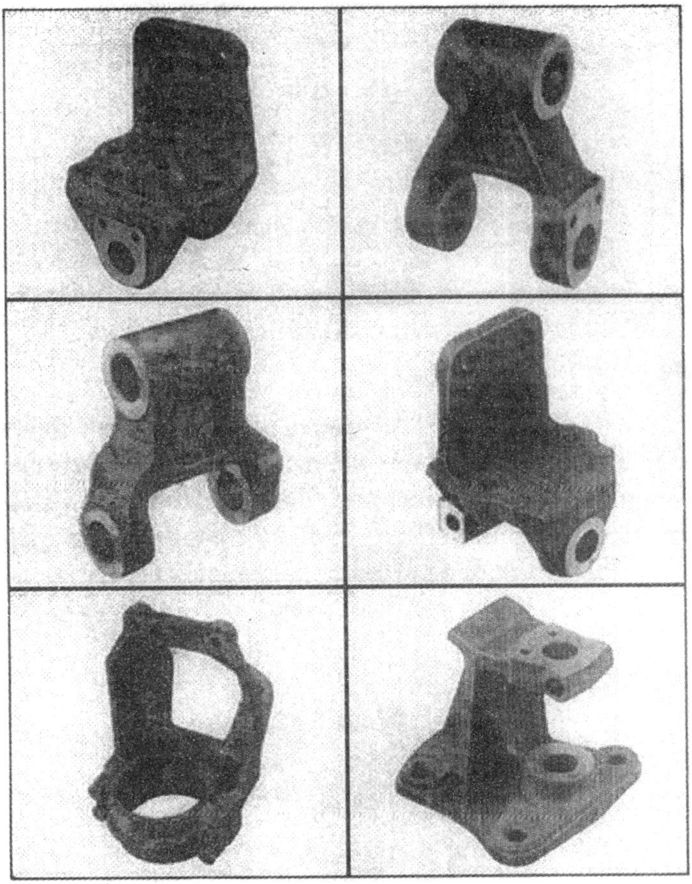

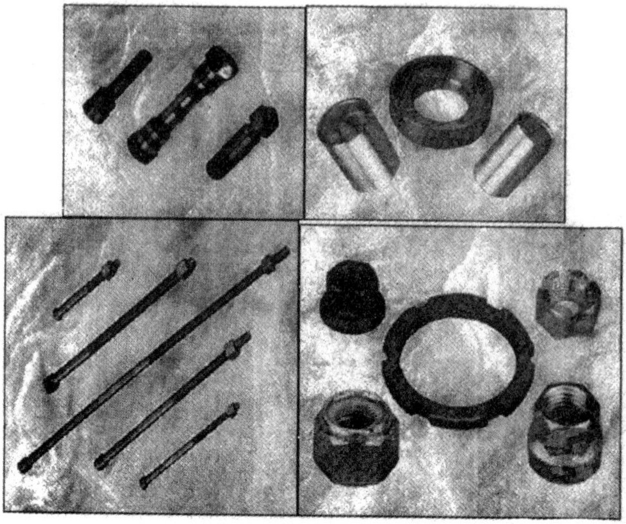

Foreign Presence of the group

Survival in today's business - world is possible if one forgets the geographical boundaries. Harbouring this principle, efforts were made in the 70's to develop overseas markets and ever since then, there is no looking back.

Some of the 20 countries in which GS group has made its presence felt

---

Holland

United Kingdom

Germany

Malaysia

Saudi Arabia

Iran

U.A.E

U.S.A.

Morocco

Egypt

Singapore

Kuwait

Kenya

Diversification

The company diversified into the field of Food. The company launched SAHIB tea.

Products of Food Division

Data Sheet

Year of Start	1948
Automotive	Automobile Components (Cast, Forged, Manufactured) Radiators, Tea, Hand Tools, Handicrafts
Total Turnover	Rs. 60 crores approx.
Domestic Turnover	55%
Foreign Turnover	45%
Compound Annual Growth Rate of Sales for last 10 years.	10.72%
Certifications	ISO 9002&9000
Stock Exchange Listings	Nil
New Ventures	Nil
Major Collaborations	Calsonic Zlanelli Radiators Ltd.UK for Radiators
Flagship Company	G.S.. Auto International Ltd.
Main Markets being served Domestic	All over India, main markets are Maharashtra, MP and UP
Foreign Market	UK, Germany, Holland, Africa

Face to Face with S. Jagat Singh, Managing Director

Mr. Jagat Singh (MD) during conversation revealed that three factors are vital to be successful in any business. First factor is mental preparedness i.e. a person should have the zeal and aspiration to succeed. This factor provides the never-ending intrinsic motivation. Second important factor is being quality conscious because quality has become a bare essential to compete in the market, either you are a quality manufacturer or you are not a manufacturer at all. Third factor is competitive pricing that GS is providing in the market place by rigorous cost cutting by means of reduced material handling, manufacturing cost and eliminating rejections despite being pitched against some very aggressive competitors.

Only real assimilation can bring real benefits. GS Group has also embraced new advances in the field of computers and information flow. GS group has distinction of being one of the few groups which are fully computerised and important functions like that of finance, PPC, Inventory Control and costing are now functioning. With more co-ordination and reports which use to take processing time of 2-3 months, like annual reports/Balance sheets, are being processed almost daily. GS Group responds quickly to such changes, in fact during first stay of IBM in India in year 1972, employees were deputed by GS for training. Presently in house training facilities are available for employees to get tech savvy.

Mr. Singh told that although conditions have improved a lot since beginning of reforms in 1991, but even today we must admit a lot of red tapism is still hindering the entrepreneurs in different ventures.

According to Mr. Jagat Singh, Lot of technical education institutions are mushrooming in Punjab. But I am not satisfied with there performance in qualitative terms. Because budding young engineers do not like to work on machines and the very fact is harming growth of technical education. Lack of practical exposure is a main problem faced by fresh engineers inducted into real manufacturing world. If one is not thorough with working and maintenance of the machine one cannot be a good technician. Students from various engineering and management institutes are provided around 6-8 weeks of industrial exposure during their professional courses. But to me only few are interested in actual learning and say 99% come just for passing time. We are ensuring that every student coming to us for summer placement gets a project to work on and only after meeting prescribed standards training completion certificates are issued. For improving standards in technical education effort must be made to acquaint both teachers as well as students the real work environment. A lot of work is unfinished in this context at least in north India, Mr. Singh remarked

Indian firms can definitely face the global competition. According to Mr. Singh GS group looks up to globalization as an opportunity rather than as a threat. Modern techniques can always help the industry to grow. The real issue is how to get different techniques and concepts into act. GS group has always responded to global challenges and presently the group is having both ISO 9002 and QS 9000 certifications to its credit. Recently 5s is being implemented in the group factories and implementation phase is almost over and the results are just wonderful and improvements have to level of 100% in each section on various counts.

Regarding "Dragon Fear" Mr. Singh remarked that not necessarily manufacturing sector of India is lagging on cost front. Recently a local firm of Ludhiana has produced a cycle, which is superior in quality and less costly as compared to Chinese version. Rather need of the hour is taking initiatives leading to cost efficiency in Indian manufacturing, which is not a difficult task

GS Group has added a new line in its existing portfolio as GS foods limited, which will be launching a new product in form of "Sahib Tea" throughout India. In our traditional line we are developing capabilities in supplying new items as OEMs. A bracket was being imported by Maruti Udyog Ltd. from Delphi Auto which was being used in AC Unit of Zen. GS Auto International has provided the same component of better quality and at a lower price. Medium size trucks are expected phase out and these will be replaced by mega and mini trucks. Our group is planning on long term basis to respond to his change and R&D department is making all the efforts to serve the OEM sector customers proactively addressing to changes in components .We are aiming for a complete Research and Development centre where latest facilities for design and drawing will be available under one roof, Mr. Singh informed.

In next 10 years GS Group would like to be leader in auto component manufacturing so we are therefore looking to expand our capacity, and we hope GS Auto will conform to 'Factory of Future" concept by adding latest technology like Computer Integrated Mfg. (CIM), Robotics, and Flexible manufacturing system with adding of latest facilities and equipment's

GS Group is abiding by its social responsibility by its involvement in education and social concern. The educational institutes being run under the patronage of the group include Guru Nanak Public School, Ramgarhia Girl's College, Ramgarhia Middle School and Ramgarhia Senior Secondary School in Ludhiana.

7

The Hero Group

Introduction: Indian Cycle Industry

With an annual production of more than 12 million bicycles, the bicycle industry in India is one of the most established the country has today. It has raised the country's position to that of the second largest bicycle manufacturer in the world, next only to China. Today not only is the Indian bicycle industry well accepted but is also widely recognized for its quality standards in international markets.

Most bicycle components and bicycle spare parts in India, except for free wheels and single piece bicycle hubs, are manufactured by the Small Scale Sector (SSIs), while the large scale units are permitted to manufacture bicycle frames, chains and rims for captive consumption. Manufacturer of complete bicycles falls within the purview of the Organized Sector. The bicycle industry is currently in the midst of making endeavors for enhanced and increased bicycle exports since the scope for export of Indian manufactured bicycles in the international market is significant. As per public reports the present level of exports falls within the range of Rs. 150 crores p.a.

A popular means of transportation in various areas of the world today, the bicycle actually evolved from a little wooden horse with a fixed front wheel in France in the 1790's. This model was improved in Germany in 1817 by Baron Karl von Drais. The model for the modern bike the "safety bicycle", was invented in England in the early 1880's, with a chain, sprocket driving rear wheel and equal sized wheels. The years that followed saw further development of the bicycle with pneumatic tires, two and three speed hub gears, and the derailleur gears, which was the last major innovation of bicycle design in the 1970's. Bicycles today offer more than just the simple pleasure of cycling. From fitness and trekking to racing, bicycles today cover a much broader spectrum of activities than in the days of their predecessors.

The Indian bicycle industry came into existence when East India Company came to Calcutta. It was at that time that the English people brought bicycle technology to India. At that time, the parts were imported, assembled into bicycles and then marketed in India. In 1953, the scenario changed entirely, when some of the noted companies like Hero and Avon were given the license to manufacture bicycles.

After almost four decades, in the post 1991 scenario, Indian industries are free to breath in the global environment. But at the same time this change has thrown up a number of challenges before the local industrial houses. In the presence of high tax rates, bureaucratic control, and poor infrastructure, the home industry finds it tough to stand upto global competition. Despite all these adversities, the cycle industry has grown to 12 million cycles a year and is growing at the rate of 11 percent per annum.

Background/Historical Perspective

Hero, a group of 15 companies, owes its success to 3D's (Dedication, Determination and Diligence).

FAMILY HIREARCHY OF HERO GROUP

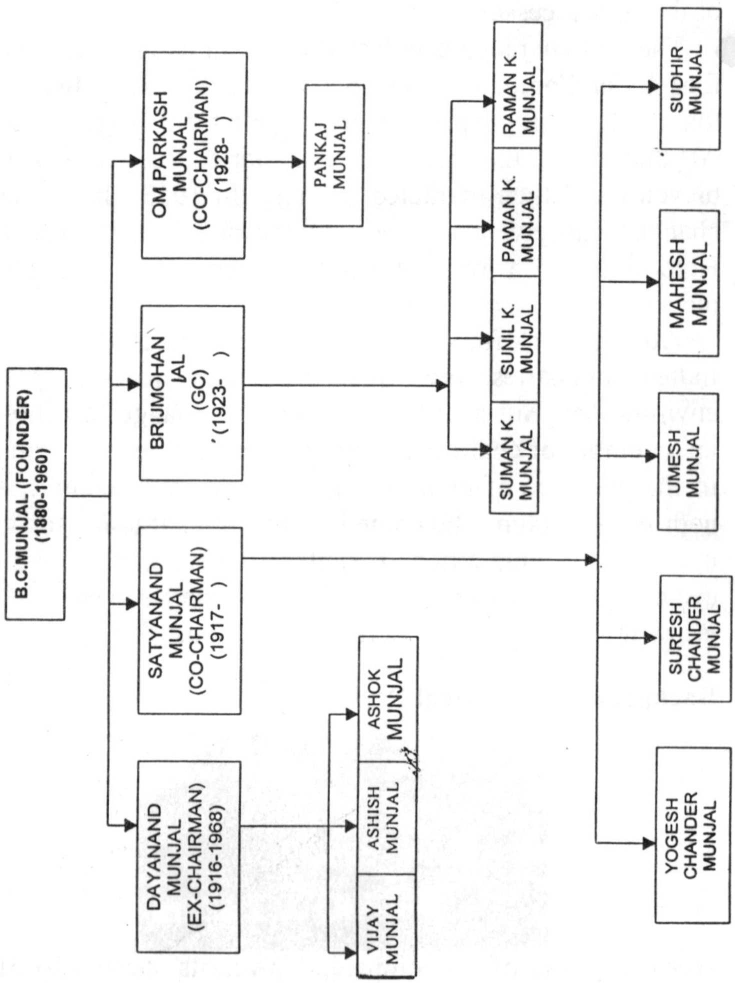

(From Left to Right): Mr. Vijay Munjal s/o Late Mr. Dayanand Munjal, Mr. Satyanand Munjal, Mr. B.M. Lall, Mr. O.P. Munjal

Hero, began its journey in India with two wheeler, more than four decades, ago in 1956. Starting as a manufacturer of bicycle components, Hero has today grown into a multi-unit, multi-product, geographically diversified group of companies. Like every success story, Hero's saga contains an element of spirit and enterprise; of achievement through grit and determination, coupled with vision and meticulous planning.

History unfolds -- In 1945 four brothers of the Munjal family started their journey by setting up their first shop of bicycle parts in Amritsar. Today the group has 15 companies including the largest cycle manufacturer, 'Hero Cycles limited', that started its operations in 1956 with a production capacity of 639 cycles/day. Presently, the company has touched the capacity of manufacturing 17,000 cycles per day.

Incorporation & Integration

With a modest beginning as supplier of bicycle

components in the early Forties, the Munjal brothers - architects of Hero -- switched over to the manufacture of bicycle parts in 1954, and finally, complete bicycles, in 1956. The flame, kindled by the founder, Mr. Dayanand Munjal (1916-1968), has not dimmed with the passage of time. In fact, three of the co-founders - Mr. Satyanand Munjal, Mr. Brijmohan Lal and Mr. O. P. Munjal continue to carry the torch and are actively involved in the day-to-day operations of the Hero Group. The saga is being continued with the same zeal by the second and third generations of the family and workers, with a spirit of enterprise, characteristic of the land where it all began - the City of Ludhiana, in Punjab, home to some of India's finest workers and entrepreneurs. Of course, much has to do with what Hero has to offer to all those who choose to work within its fold. Here job security, growth opportunity and respect are the unspoken, yet understood aspects of every man's package.

The Hero Group began with a simple philosophy: to provide excellent transportation to the common man, at a price he could easily afford.

It is this spirit, which drives Hero even today; the dream of providing total satisfaction in all its spheres of activity. To consumers, in excellent products at an affordable price; to employees, in a fine quality of life; and to business associates, in a total sense of belonging.

The prime mover for Hero has been engineering satisfaction, which is a way of life and part of the work-culture of the Group. This has driven Hero to seek newer avenues and technologies, to transform them into products that have fulfilled the Hero dream, and catapulted the Group into the Guinness Book of World Records as the largest maker of bicycles in the world. Hero is also the largest manufacturer of 100cc motorcycles in India, and has a substantial presence in mopeds and auto-ancilliaries.

Yet changing consumer needs and newer technologies provide fresh challenges every day, and at Hero the wheels of progress continue to turn...

The search for excellence led to the creation of several companies by the Hero Group. Companies that maintained the ethos of perfect quality, which helped the Group attain its global stature and self-reliance in the entire manufacturing process. Keeping the wheels of progress turning are the individual companies of the Hero Group, each an independent profit centre, each a success story in its own right. The Hero Group has also helped promote more than 300 ancillaries which meet its needs of smaller components, and more than 3,500 dealer outlets, each with its complement of trained mechanics and workers.

The Hero Group's forays into the overseas markets pioneered Indian exports in the bicycle segment as early as 1963. A move prompted, essentially, by the need to remain attuned to the global marketplace.

Mission of the Hero Group

1. Maintaining leadership by keeping demanding customers satisfied with innovative products that are consistent in quality and reliability.
2. By converting challenges into opportunities by initiating change.
3. Improving the quality.

Foreign Presence

While initial exports were restricted to Africa and the Middle East, today more than 50 percent of the Group's bicycle exports meet the demands of sophisticated markets in Europe and the U.S. Much of this is a result of appropriate product development and excellent quality that Hero has to offer. There has also been a steady upgradation of technologies and the setting up of special units, like Gujarat Cycles Limited, to meet stringent international standards. But exports have gone beyond cycles and their components. The success of the Hero Majestic moped did not remain confined to Indian shores. Finding enthusiastic buyers across the world, it became the largest exported moped from India.

The Hero Puch is perhaps the first Indian two-wheeler to be homologated abroad (in Spain) and has assembly plants in Mauritius and Egypt. Today Hero is the largest exporter of two-wheelers in India, besides being the fastest growing Indian two-wheeler company. The search for excellence knows no boundaries-global or otherwise. In 1983, it led Hero to form a joint venture (in technical and financial participation) with one of the world's largest automotive makers, Honda Motor Company Ltd. of Japan, for the manufacture of 100cc motorcycles in India.

A joint venture with Showa Manufacturing Co., Japan, for the production of front forks and shock absorbers for two-wheelers and four-wheelers followed. The Group also ventured into a technical consultancy agreement with Steyr Daimler Puch of Austria for the manufacture of the 65cc, Porsche-design mini-motorcycles.

The Group has also been acquiring the services of foreign consultants and experts for identification and development of business opportunities and assistance in technical upgradation. The entire range of bicycle products of Gujarat Cycles Ltd., Baroda, was developed with German expertise and the entire software for bicycle parts was developed using Japanese know-how. Such technology assimilation through wide sourcing is a regular feature at Hero.

Hero: A New Perspective

A thorough understanding of fast-changing consumer behaviour, new market segments and product opportunities, and a marketing mix sensitive to changing customer needs, form the core of Hero's marketing strategy and philosophy.

It is basically a customer-driven company. A nation-wide dealer network comprising of over 3,500 bicycle dealers, 350 dealers for mopeds and 225 franchise holders for motorcycles, ensures convenient access to the Group's products across the country. With a deep sense of belonging to the Hero fraternity, the Group's dealers have catalyzed growth and act as a strong bridge between the customers and the Group.

Quality at Hero is not just modern plants and equipment, it is an everyday discipline. It is technology seeped in experience that spans nearly four decades. It is an attitude that masters the challenge of growth and change. By tradition, conformance to quality at Hero begins on the shop floor, with every worker ensuring at each stage of manufacturing, that nothing faulty passes through his hands. Today, quality is ensured from steel processing to the finished product. Each component goes through numerous tests at the stages of design, raw material procurement, and, of course, during the manufacturing process.

Constant technology upgradation ensures that the Group stays in the global mainstream, and maintains its competitive edge. Besides the improved quality control methods that came about with every foreign collaboration, the Group also employs the services of independent experts from around the world to assist in new design and production processes. But tradition remains uppermost. Control on quality still begins on the shop floor, a matter of pride for the worker. In view of the radically divergent needs of the international bicycle markets, the Hero Group promoted Gujarat Cycles Limited as a 100 percent export-oriented unit (EOU).

A joint venture with the State-owned Gujarat Industrial Investment Corporation, it has helped the Group to cater to the needs of sophisticated markets like the United States and Germany, and is now poised for entry into the markets of the UK and Australia.

The company believes in change at all levels with the passage of time. The company constantly upgrades its state-of-the-art plants, and new management strategies and techniques are welcome at all the stages. The company has entered into the new business of Information Technology Enabled Services and Financial Services.

Keeping in view the tremendous growth and business opportunity in Customer Relationship Management and Call Centre industry in India, the company is entering into new business alliances with Briggs and Stratton, manufacturer of engines, and First Ring Inc, call centre services and customer management services provider of USA. The group is also trying to have a tie-up with the largest insurance company in the world for entry in the financial sector. As far as social responsibility of the group is concerned, Munjal brothers have shown their care for the society by opening professional academic institutes, hospitals, social welfare organizations, and clubs, where various kind of facilities are provided to the people. Though LPG (Liberalization, Privatization and Globalization) factor has influenced the whole economy, the HERO GROUP is aware of all the changes. The group is ready to combat the growing challenges of global competition. The company has already diversified its operations into various sectors by collaborating with various companies.

Foreign Collaborations

Hero Honda Motors Limited

Hero Group collaborated with Honda Motors of Japan and set up state-of-the-art plant to produce internationally accepted range of motorcycles in 1984 at New Delhi. The group is headed by Mr. Pawan Kant Munjal s/o Mr. Brij Mohan Lal. The finest and most demanding product of this group has been CBZ 156 CC motorbike.

Munjal Showa Limited

In 1985 the group collaborated with Showa Manufacturing Company of Japan, a pioneer in manufacturing of Shock absorbers. The plant is headed by Mr. Yogesh Chander Munjal s/o Mr. Satyanand Munjal and is located at Gurgaon. These shock absorbers are exported to big manufacturers of fourwheelers in Japan and this group has established its name over there.

Hero Briggs and Stratton Limited

In 1998 a joint venture between the Hero Group and Briggs and Stratton, USA took place to manufacture engines for two wheelers. The plant was set up at New Delhi and is headed by Mr. Sunil Kant Munjal s/o Mr. B.M. Lall. Very soon the plant will start functioning to its full capacity.

First Ring Inc., USA

This group has acquired a major stake in this company and is in the business of providing Call Center Services and Customer Management Services. The group is making efforts to enter into financial services sector and Call Centers in the year 2003. Mr. Sunil Kant Munjal, s/o Mr. Brij Mohan Munjal, is heading this organization.

Group Companies

Bicycles

1. Hero Cycles (Ludhiana / Mangli / Chennai)

Hero Cycles Ltd. started functioning in 1956. Four Munjal Brothers - Dayanand Munjal, Satyanand Munjal, Brij Mohan Lal and Om Parkash Munjal - started this venture with the hope of capturing the business market of India and the World. The first plant was set up at G.T. Road, Ludhiana. In the year 2000, two were setup, one at Chennai and the other at Nichi Mangli, Chandigarh Road, Ludhiana. Mr. Satyanand Munjal, Mr. O.P. Munjal, Mr Suresh Munjal and Mr. Vijay Munjal, based in Ludhiana are looking after the company. Mr. Brij Mohan Lall handles the Chennai plant. The company has a manufacturing capacity of 17,000 cycles per day. It has a strong dealer network of 3500 dealers. The company believes in the policy of commitment to change. More emphasis is given on the quality of the product, skill-improvement of the workers, upgradation of machines, and continuous evaluation of manufacturing processes. HERO RANGER has been the most successful product of the group. It has over 19 models in the kids segment including the latest Cadet, Li Angel, Kidd, Piranha, Sparky, Active and Hero Buzz, which is the first bike, designed by CAD.

Hero Cycles Limited (Unit II)

2. **Hero Cycles Unit-II (Sahibabad, Uttar Pradesh)**

In 1988, the second unit of Hero Cycles was setup to meet the increasing demand of the product. Statistics for the year 1988 show that there was an increase of 40%in the demand for the product in the domestic market, and 26% increase in the export demand. The plant has a capacity of producing 3,500 cycles a day. The plant is equipped with state-of-the-art technology with centralized cold forging facility to manufacture pedals and axles.

Hero Cycles Limited was the first company of the Group, and continues to remain the flagship unit. Starting with a modest figure of 25 bicycles per day in 1956 at Ludhiana, the Company extended its wings to establish its second unit in 1988 at Sahibabad (U.P.). Today the combined production of the two units is more than 20,500 bicycles a day. In terms of complete bicycles, Hero Cycles is a clear leader in the domestic market, besides having a fair representation in over 60 international markets. The wide product range caters to the entire spectrum of buyers, and includes roadsters, racers, and the latest all-terrain and city bicycles. Massive in its dimensions, the Hero Cycles plant at Ludhiana also houses the centralised rim-making facility for the entire range of Hero two-wheelers. Besides, all major components, it has in-house facilities for making pedals, handlebars, chainwheels, brakes and saddles.

3. Gujarat Cycles Limited (Vadodara, Gujarat)

This unit is headed by Mr. Sudhir Munjal. The plant was established in 1990 to cater to the need of auto-parts in the Indian market. The unit has specialization in the manufacturing of Auto Rim and Mufflers. With State-of-Art -Technology, the plant has been successful in delivering quality products to the domestic as well as export market.

User Industries

Mopeds, Scooters & Motor Cycles , Car Components, Jeep Components, Truck Components, Tractor Components, Bicycle and Components, Automobiles, Railways, Electrical Machinery, White Goods, Industrial Machinery, Office Equipment, Packaging Materials, Pipes & Tubes, etc.

Components

Rockman Cycle Industries Limited

4. Rockman Cycles Industries Limited (Ludhiana)

Rockman Cycle Industries Limited was founded at a time when there was an extreme scarcity of bicycle chains in the country. Today the company is manufacturing more than 45,000mts of single and multi speed chains on daily basis. Around 25% of the product is exported to European countries. The company has got ISO 9002 certification. It has also entered into the business of Motorcycle chains and hubs. This group is headed by Mr. Suman Munjal s/o Mr. Brij Mohan Lall.

The Company manufactures about 25,000 single- and multi-speed chains everyday. In 1964, the Company started manufacture of bicycle hubs, and today it has a daily production of about 50,000 pieces. Rockman products have become well-known in the bicycle industry in India and abroad and cater to the needs of some of the finest bicycle manufacturers in Europe.Equipped with the best technology for its requirements, the Company also has its own design and machine manufacturing section, nickel plating plants, and a fully-equipped heat treatment department.

Highway Cycles Industries Limited

5. Highway Cycle Industries (Ludhiana)

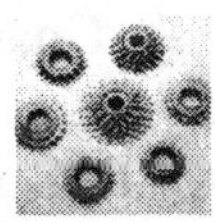

Highway Cycles was established in 1971 to cater to the demand for freewheels for the bicycle industry. Mr. Umesh Munjal, s/o Mr. Satyanand Munjal, is heading this unit, which started Initially manufacturing single-speed free-wheels. The Company began production of multi-speed freewheels in 1978, essentially to cater to the demands of foreign buyers. Today, the company has a capacity of 45,000 freewheels per day. The company is producing multi-speed, index and non-index freewheels to meet the demand of foreign markets as well. The product is being exported to Germany, Italy, France, South Africa and South America. Presently, the Company exports 100 percent of its multi-speed and 30 percent of its single-speed freewheels. The Company, however, did not restrict its technical expertise to a single function, and today designs and manufactures special purpose machines for all the companies in the Hero Group.

6. Munjal Auto Components (Gurgaon)

In 1999 a division of Gujarat Cycles Limited was established, named Munjal Auto, to produce a wide array of high precision, near net shape forging parts for automobiles. Japanese technology is used for manufacturing of this product. This unit is headed by Mr. Sudhir Munjal s/o Mr. Satyanand Munjal.

7. Munjal Showa (Gurgaon)

In 1985 the group collaborated with Showa Manufacturing Company of Japan, a pioneer in manufacturing of shock absorbers. The plant is headed by Mr. Yogesh Chander Munjal, s/o Mr. Satyanand Munjal, and is located at Gurgaon. These shock absorbers are exported to big manufacturers of fourwheelers in Japan. This product has established its name in Japan as well.

The Company, since its inception has been a trail-blazer for achieving impressive all-round growth. In a short span of time, the Company achieved phenomenal success. The Company's state-of-the-art Shock Absorbers, Front Fork, Struts and Window Balancers, Gas Springs have become symbols of Quality and complete reliability for popular TWO AND FOUR WHEELER vehicles. The ultra modern plant is situated in Gurgaon (Haryana). The Company's products conform to highest standard of Quality, Safety and Dependability. The Company's work culture is based on Quality Foundation. Every Component is put through gruelling technical and endurance tests to ensure flawless finish and performance. MSL Shock Absorbers can withstand more than two million cycle tests, far exceeding ISI's stipulation of one million cycles.

The coveted QS 9000 and ISO 9001 was conferred on Munjal Showa Ltd. in 1997 for DESIGN AND DEVELOPMENT AND MANUFACTURE OF FRONT FORKS, SHOCK ABSORBERS, STRUTS AND GAS STRUTS. It was a significant achievement, which confirmed recognition to the Quality and Systems Internationally. In the past, the Company had received NATIONAL SAFETY AWARD IN 1992, & ISO 9002 in 1996. The Company's Products enjoy wide patronage and serve as Original Equipment to vehicles like Maruti 800cc Car, LHD for Export, Omni, Esteem, Zen, Honda City (Car), Hero Honda (Motorcycle), Kinetic Honda (Scooter), Bajaj Kawasaki (Motorcycle), Hero Puch (Moped), and Hero Majestic (Moped), etc.

8. Hero Briggs and Stratton (New Delhi)

In 1998 a joint venture between the Hero Group and Briggs and Stratton, USA, took place to manufacture engines for two wheelers. The plant was set up at New Delhi headed by Mr. Sunil Kant Munjal, s/o Mr. B.M. Lall.

Motor Cycles

Majestic Auto Limited

9. Majestic Auto Limited (Ludhiana)

Hero Majestic, is a very popular moped among Indian citizens. The answer to the rapidly escalating fuel prices in the country came in the form of the Hero Majestic range of mopeds in the year 1978. The company is also in the business of manufacturing health equipments like steppers, joggers and Allegro. Mr. Mahesh Munjal, s/o Mr Satyanand Munjal, is heading this unit.

Within a few years, Hero Majestic became a household name in the country, and by 1983, Majestic Auto Limited was the country's leading manufacturer of mopeds. Hero Majestic Mopeds have found great acceptance in the overseas markets as well, including countries of Africa, North & South America, Europe and the far & middle East and are homologated in Europe & USA.

Majestic Auto Ltd. is continuously working to upgrade the performance of its three existing mopeds, viz., Panther, Gizmo & Ankur, and to make them eco-friendly. The company also manufactures and exports Hero Allegro exerbikes, steppers and joggers, the well accepted market leaders in fitness equipment.

Hero Honda Motors Limited

10. Hero Honda Motor (New Delhi)

Hero Group collaborated with Honda Motors of Japan and set up state-of-the-art plant to produce internationally accepted range of motorcycles in 1984 at New Delhi. This unit is headed by Mr. Pawan Kant Munjal s/o Mr. Brij Mohan Lal. The finest and most demanding product of this group has been the **CBZ 156 CC bike**.

A rich background of producing high value products, at a reasonable price, led the world's largest manufacturer of motocycles to collaborate with the world's largest bicycle manufacturer. It was this affinity in working cultures of Honda Motor Company of Japan, and the Hero Group that resulted in the setting up of Hero Honda Motors Ltd.

A relationship so harmonious that Hero Honda has managed to achieve indigenisation of over 95 percent, a Honda record worldwide. Hero Honda is today the largest-selling Indian motorcycle and the most fuel-efticient in its category, a comment on the Hero Group's foresight, and another classic example of providing the customer with excellence that is self-evident.

Excellent marketing also helped Hero Honda establish itself as an intelligent purchase. Tactical promotions helped highlight the need for fuel conservation, mobile workshops gave Hero Honda owners a plus over others in the deep interiors of the country, and safety riding courses placed the motorcycle in a league distinct from the conventional.

Financial services helped facilitate purchase, as did an efficient dealer network across the country. Well-entrenched in the domestic market, Hero Honda Motors Ltd. turned its attention overseas, and exports have since been steadily on the rise. Over the years, the Company has received its share of accolades, including the National Productivity Council's Award (1990-91), and the Economic Times - Harvard Business School Association of India Award, against 200 contenders. Aware of its social obligations, the Company operates a mobile dispensary van in the service of those living within a 10 km radius of its plant, and also conducts eye-camps each year for cataract operations on a charitable basis. Hero Honda Motors Ltd. has also established the Raman Kant Foundation, a trust to work exclusively in the area of sociocultural and educational development.

Hero Motors

11. Hero Motors (Sahibabad)

In 1988 Hero Motors was established in technical collaboration with Steyr Daimler Puch of Austria. Hero Puch is the product of this group, and has been very popular among Indians. At present the company is in the process of manufacturing Hero Winner Scooters. A joint venture of Hero Group and Briggs and Stratten, USA, has enabled Hero Motors to equip its two-wheelers with the latest and best engines. The group is headed by Mr . Pankaj Munjal, MD, s/o Mr. Om Parkash Munjal

In a competitive environment, Hero's quest for a low-budget, fuel-efficient and environment-friendly two-wheeler, led Hero Motors to enter into a technical collaboration with Steyr Daimler Puch of Austria. The entry of the Hero Puch, a Porsche design, mini-motorcycle marked a new chapter in the two-wheeler scenario of the country - a vehicle that combined the power and ease of a motorcycle and the economy of a moped.

Hero Motors commenced production of Hero Puch in October 1988 with 95 percent indigenisation. The product was soon being exported to developed countries of Europe with its homologation in Spain, besides having assembly plants in Mauritius and Egypt; proud firsts for any Indian company. Today Hero Puch mini-motorcycles can also be seen in Paraguay, Mexico, Argentina, Turkey and Holland.

Castings

11. Munjal Castings

Munjal castings were set up in 1981 as a partnership firm belonging to the Hero Group. It supplies Aluminium Die Casted components for the Hero Majestic mopeds, bicycles, and generator markets. Die casting plant is fully equipped with metallurgical laboratory.

12. Sunbeam Castings

Sunbeam castings was founded in 1987 to cater to the needs of the automobile industry, It is the largest die casting company in India with a capacity of 500 mt. The Plant is equipped with the latest machinery, it is the leading manufacturer of aluminium automotive die castings. Apart from Hero Honda and Hero motors, Sunbeam is manufacturer to many Indian and foreign companies. Maruti Udyog Ltd, Munjal Showa Ltd, Kinetic Motors Ltd, Ford motor company of USA, Chrysler Dailmer Benz AG of Germany, are a few of them. The group is headed by Mr. Ashok Munjal, MD s/o Mr. Dayanand Munjal.

Munjal & Sunbeam Casting

MUNJAL & SUNBEAM CASTINGS

This unit is engaged in the manufacture of Die Castings of Aluminium and Zinc Based alloys in Pressure, Low Pressure and Gravity Die Casting processes. The increasing demand for non-ferrous metal castings in bicycle and automotive segments led to the establishment of Munjal Castings in the year 1980. The Company meets a wide spectrum of needs, ranging from bicycle for Hero Cycles, Mopeds for Majestic Auto, and Generator markets, to other turnkey assignments. In 1983 when the group collaborated with Honda Motors,

Japan, to manufacture 100cc Motorcycles with the brand name HERO HONDA, it led to the establishment of Sunbeam Castings in Gurgaon, Haryana, in the year 1987. The main objectives for establishment of Sunbeam Castings was to indigenise the castings which were being imported from Japan. The Company was able to fulfill the objectives of indigenisation within a span of 4 years. Simultaneously, Sunbeam Castings developed die castings for another Group vehicle, Hero Puch, which is manufactured by Hero Motors (A Unit of Majestic Auto Ltd.) formed in collaboration with Styre Daimler Puch of Austria.

Seeing the strengths and capabilities of Sunbeam, Maruti Udyog Ltd. (A company formed in collaboration with SUZUKI MOTORS, JAPAN for manufacture of Cars from 800cc to 1300cc) approached this unit to develop some of their intricate castings. For some of the components Sunbeam is the single source supplier to Maruti Udyog Ltd. With the increase in market demand, the company kept on adding machineries. The unit which was started with a meager capacity to produce 500MT of Die Cast Components, today has an installed capacity of producing 5400MT of components. Sunbeam and Munjal Castings has got 34 Pressure Die Casting Machines ranging from 80 ton to 1300 tons. Two 1300 ton and one 840 ton, short control machine has been imported from Buhler, Switzerland, and is fully automatic, 32 custom built Gravity Die Casting Machines and two low Pressure Die Casting machines.

The Company has got complete facilities of Die Design, Die making, Alloy making, Die Casting, Heat-treatment, Machining, Painting of components, under single roof. They have CAD / CAM facilities with CNC Milling Machines to develop intricate dies in their Tool room. To further strengthen the Tool Room, the company has recently added three CNC Milling machines from Deckel Maho, Germany. Sunbeam Casting has its own Research and Development Centre approved by Govt. of India with sophisticated equipments. Direct Reading Spectrometer THERMO JARREL ASH, (U.S.A) 181, ATOMIC ABSORPTION SPECTROMETER A.A. SCAN 1 THERMO JARREL ASH, IMAGE ANALYZER, RADIOGRAPHIC CAMERA, ETC, to name a few. Recently a Piston manufacturing line has been set-up with indigenous technology. The machines are to manufacture A Pistons having dia ranging from 40mm to 90mm.

After meeting the requirements of the Indian Automobile Giants in the two wheeler and four wheeler segments, the company has got ambitious plans for exports of die castings in the World Automobile markets.

Services

13. Hero Corporate Services Limited

Hero Corporate Services Ltd. was set up in 1995. The company was incorporated with an objective to provide corporate services in the field of finance, HRD, IT and strategic planning.

14. Hero Financial and Leasing Limited

The group is planning to enter into financial services. The group has collaborated with First Ring Inc., USA, to start with financial services. The project is under consideration and is expected to be launched in near future.

15. About Hero Exports

Established in 1993 as a Trading Company of the Group, Hero Exports has since been recognised by the Government of India as a Trading House. Currently, the company is exporting a wide range of products including:

Bicycle Components
Basmati & Non-Basmati Rice
Pliers & Cutters
Spanners, Pliers & Wrenches
Hammers, Screwdrivers & Hacksaws
Lubrication equipment & Clamps
Garden Tools

Hero Exports has been able to establish enduring relationship/association with the clients overseas as a result of their unrelenting policy of supplying quality products conforming to international standards at reasonable prices, coupled with efficient and timely deliveries. The Company, as a result of its deep-rooted desire to be counted amongst the leading players in the field of exports, has been able to build an envious position amongst its contemporaries.

Awards & Certifications

1. Mr. Brij Mohan Lall, Chairman, was presented the prestigious Shri Jehangir Ghandy Medal for industrial peace.
2. Mr. O. P. Munjal, Co-Chairman & CEO received the Punjab Rattan award from H.E. Lt. Gen. J.F.R. Jacob (retd.).

Certifications:

ISO 9002 (Det Norske Veritas Quality System Certificate)

Face to Face with Mr. Satyanand Munjal, Co-Chairman, HERO

During a conversation with us, Mr. Satya Nand Munjal, Co-Chairman, Hero Group, said that the main strengths of the group were: State of the art technology, Brand Name & Customer trust and the secret of success was that they were changing with time. **Mr. Munjal said this had been the fact for centuries that no business could grow if it ignored the changes in the world, they were proud to accept that HERO always changed with the changes in time.** Besides consistent hard work, honesty towards customers, clients and employees, the company believes in doing ethical business. We are God fearing and believe that honesty can lead us to such a height of success which otherwise can not be achieved.

Talking about the LPG (Liberalisation, Privatisation and Globalisation) factor Mr. Munjal showed his firm confidence in Indian firms and said Indian industry was competitive enough to face challenges of globalization. India is a big market which carries large scope of consumption. To compete with the challenge of globalization, it is pre requisite to be more competitive and to be able to change with the passage of time.

Mr. Munjal stated that their business had benefited a lot by using information technology. All the departments of HERO are fully computerized and interconnected. With the help of IT department it had been possible to get increased speed of information flow, implementation of MIS & proper handling of accounts. Proper care of all the systems being implemented is taken with the help of a separate IT Department. By computerizing our business we are getting the advantages of speedy flow of information, proper handling of accounts and properly implementing Management Information System in the organization. Hero Cycles have implemented ERP i.e. Enterprise Resource Planning, which had helped them to operate more efficiently and effectively and also getting cost advantage not only to the company but also to their customers and suppliers. We have implemented SAP also in the units.

Discussing about human resources, he said that it was as important as other functional areas such as Marketing, Finance, Production, etc. Right from the start, the credit of their success is attributed to the employees of the company. The group believes in satisfying its employees by fulfilling their expectations and also expects the same from them for the business group. The group believes in the philosophy that employees are as important as the customers.

While talking about the management education being provided by educational institutes, with special reference to the regional institutes, Mr. Munjal said that for better performance by students as managers and other technical employees, the students should be given more and more practical exposure. They should undergo rigorous practical training in companies.

When asked about the initiatives taken by the group regarding its social responsibilities, Mr. Munjal said that the group believed in giving due care to the society. Considering this as a responsibility, the group itself had taken a number of initiatives such as running BCM School, R. S. Model School, Hero DMC Heart Institute, and participation in various social welfare organizations and committees. Hero group is concerned for its employees, society and the environment. The company provides healthy working environment and in-house medical facilities for its employees. The HERO group contributes a part of its earnings towards welfare of the society, it contributes actively to community development, charity and promotion of sports. Welfare activities are not only confined to their employees but also for the whole community. Special emphasis is laid on eco-friendly manufacturing processes for the protection of the environment.

Talking about the future of Ludhiana industry, especially with emergence of low cost competition from firms of China, Mr. Munjal said that despite recession in the market these days, the future of the Ludhiana industry is very bright. However, it will have to take care of a few things like Quality work, Focused approach, Change with time, Regular supervision, implementation of successful management practices and policies, and so on.

Mr. Munjal told us about the future plans of the group these include diversifying to Financial Services, Call centre, Auto Rim/parts, Cycle parts for American industry, and Corporate Services.

When asked how Mr. Munjal visualized his group after 10 years, he said that at present they were having 15 factories. Their aim was that all these factories should flourish in the future. They are regularly emphasizing two critical aspects i.e. what can be better than the existing, and how can they be better than what they were now. We are aiming to improve continuously by cooperation and coordination of employees. Bicycle is a low price product. Foreign companies were not interested in producing cycles as it requires more investment in manufacturing. They expected the group to flourish in the coming times. Our main strengths are state-of-the-art technology being used, brand, and the trust of the customers. They expected to grow on the basis of these strengths.

About Flagship Company of HERO Group – (Hero Honda Motors)

Hero Honda is presently the largest two-wheeler companies in India. Hero Honda Motors Ltd. touched a sale of 1,029,591 motorcycles in 2000-2001. This figure was

HHML's target for 2004-2005. A target being achieved so much ahead of time speaks of unprecedented success.

Brij Mohan Lall, chairman and managing director, HHML, has always viewed business in context of the value it delivers to the society in general. He says, 'if you fix a goal and implement your strategy sincerely you can achieve anything. Everyone, from vendors to floor workers in Hero Honda, has put in a very dedicated effort to achieve this.'

Both its plants at Daruhera and Gurgaon in Haryana have been working with modern 4-stroke engine technology cranking out 2400 & 1800 motorcycles a day respectively. Hero Hondia's current models, namely Splendor, Passion, CBZ and Street Smart are now in the market and its latest offering is P-25. Hero Honda believes that employee involvement is important. Daily meetings, suggestion schemes and weekly reviews keep every employee involved.

Products/Services

S.No	Company Name	Year of start	Main Products Operating	Location
1.	Hero Cycles	1956	Cycles	Ludhiana
2.	Rockman Cycle Industries Ltd	1961	Single & Multispeed Chains	Ludhiana
3.	Highway Cycles	1971	Freewheels	Ludhiana
4.	Majestic Auto Ltd.	1978	Moped & Health Equipments	Ludhiana
5.	Munjal Castings	1981	Aluminium Die Casted Components	Ludhiana
6.	Hero Honda Motors Ltd.	1984	Motor Cycles	New Delhi
7.	Munjal Showa Ltd.	1985	Shock Absorbers	Gurgaon
8.	Sunbeam Castings	1987	Aluminium Automotive Die Casted Components	Gurgaon
9.	Hero Motors	1988	Hero Puch, Hero Winner Scooters	Sahibabad
10.	Hero Cycles Unit-II	1988	Cycles	Sahibabad
11.	Gujrat Cycles Ltd.	1988	Auto parts	Baroda
12.	Hero Cold Rolling Mills	1990	Steel Processing	Ludhiana
13.	Hero Corporate Services Ltd.	1996	Provides Services	New Delhi
14.	Hero Briggs & Stratton	1998	Engines for two wheelers	New Delhi
15.	Munjal Auto Components	1999	Forging parts for Automobile	Gurgaon

16.	Hero Cycles Ltd.	2000	Cycles	Chennai
17.	Hero Cycles Ltd.	2000	Cycles	Ludhiana
18.	Hero Financial & Leasing Ltd.	In process		

Business Bicycles	**Hero Cycles Limited** Established in 1956 Ludhiana Product : Bicycles	**Hero Cycles Limited (Unit II)** Established in 1988 Sahibabad Product : Bicycles	**Gujarat Cycles Limited** Established in 1988 Baroda Product : Bicycles
Business Auto-Two Wheelers	**Hero Honda Motors Limited** Established in 1983 New Delhi Product : Motorcycles Collaborator : Honda Motor Co. Ltd., Japan	**Majestic Auto Limited** Established in 1978 Ludhiana Product : Mopeds & Fitness Equipment	**Hero Motors** (A division of Majestic Auto Limited) Established in 1988 Ghaziabad Product : Mini-motorcycles Collaborator: Steyr Daimler Puch, Austria Product: Scooters, Collaborators: Malguti, Italy.
Business Bicycle and Auto Components	**Rockman Cycle Industries Limited** Established in 1960 Ludhiana Product : Automotive & Bicycle Chains; Steel & Aluminium Hubs.	**Highway Cycle Industries Limited** Established in 1971 Ludhiana Product : Freewheels & Special Machine Tools	**Munjal Showa Limited** Established in 1985 Gurgaon Product : Shock Absorbers Collaborator : Showa Manufacturing Co. Japan
Business Castings	**Munjal Castings** Established in 1981 Ludhiana Product : Non-	**Sunbeam Castings** Established in 1987	**Hero Cycles-Cold Rolling Division** Established in 1990

and Steel	ferrous Castings	Gurgaon Product : Non-ferrous Castings	Ludhiana Product : Cold Rolled Steel Sheets and Coils
Business Services	**Hero Exports** Established in 1993 Ludhiana Product: International Trading Company dealing in Commodoties & Engineering Items	**Hero Corporate Services** Established in 1995 New Delhi Product: Corporate Services in Finance, HRD, IT & Strategic Planning	**Munjal Sales Corporation** Established in 1975 Ludhiana Product: Sole Selling Agents of Bicycles and Bicycles Parts for India.

Addresses Of Various Group Companies

HERO CYCLES LIMITED
Hero Nagar, G.T. Road
Ludhiana - 141003, (Punjab) India
Tel.: +91-161-539448 to 52
Fax : +91-161-539475/539478
Tlx.: 0386-405.HEPX IN
Email: infor.hero@herogroup.com,
info@herocycles.com

HERO CYCLES-COLD
ROLLING DIVISION
G.T. Road, Ludhiana - 141003 (Punjab) India
Tel.: +91-161-539453/539454
Fax : +91-161-539455
Email: systems.crd@herogroup.com

HIGHWAY CYCLE INDUSTRIES LIMITED
698-Industrial Area B
1. Ludhiana - 141003, (Punjab) India
Tel.: +91-161- 531624 to 26
Fax : +91-161-532243
Email:highway@herogroup.com

2. Vill.Nandpur
Near Sahnewal,G.T.Road,
Ludhiana

HERO CYCLES LIMITED (UNIT II)
Plot No. 8-A, Site IV
Industrial Area, Sahibabad
Distt. Ghaziabad, U.P., India
Tel.: +91-575-770980 to 83
Fax : +91-575-770928
Email:
mktg @herogrp.sprintrpg.ems.vsnl.net.in

MAJESTIC AUTO LIMITED
C-48 Focal Point
Ludhiana - 141010, (Punjab) India
•Tel.: +91-161-670233 to 37
Fax : +91-161-672790
Email:
export.mal@herogrp.sprintrpg.ems.vsnl.net.in

ROCKMAN CYCLE
INDUSTRIES LIMITED
A-7 Focal Point
Ludhiana-141010, (Punjab) India
Tel.: +91-161-670701 to 03
Fax : +91-161-670700
Email: rockman@herogroup.com

Tel: 0161 - 844730,845029-30
Fax: 0161 – 844729

MUNJAL CASTINGS
730 industrial Area B
Ludhiana - 141003, (Punjab) India
Tel.:+91-161-535126, 533896
Fax: +91-161-532372
Email:
general.mc@herogrp.sprintrpg.ems.vsnl.net.in

HERO HONDA MOTORS LIMITED
34 Basant Lok, Community Centre
Vasant Vihar, New Delhi - 110057, India
Tel.: +91-11-6142451 to 59
Fax : +91-11-6143321/6143198
WORKS:
69 Km Stone,
New Delhi-Jaipur Highway
Daruhera - 121 106
(Haryana) India
Email:hhonda@nda.vsnl.net.in

MUNJAL SHOWA LIMITED
9-10 Maruti Area
Gurgaon - 122015, (Haryana) India
Tel.:+91-124 - 340427 to 29, 341001 to 03
Fax:+91-124 - 341346 / 341359
Email: munjal.globalnet.ems.vsnl.net.in

HERO MOTORS
601 International Trade Tower
Nehru Place
New Delhi - 110 019, India
Tel.:+91-11-621660 to 62,6216666 to 67,6216699
Fax : +91-11 - 6471230 / 6475194
Works: works@heromotors.com
Email:
mis.del@herogrp.sprintrpg.ems.vsnl.net.in
(+10th Km Stone, G.T. Road,P.O. Dujana)
Tel: +91- 575-392109,392122 to 25
Fax: +91- 575 - 700686

GUJARAT CYCLES LIMITED
3 B, Ramakrishan Chambers
Productivity Road, Alkapuri
Baroda-390005, (Gujarat) India
Tel.: +91-265-334401 to 04
Fax : +91-265-331924
Email:
info.gcl@herogrp.sprintrpg.ems.vsnl.net.in

SUNBEAM CASTINGS
38/6 km Stone
Delhi-Jaipur Highway
Narsingpur - 122001,(Haryana) India
Tel.:+91-124-372075, 372614, 371756
Fax : +-124-371010

HERO EXPORTS
Hero Nagar, G.T. Road
Ludhiana - 141 003, (Punjab) INDIA
Tel.: +91-161-539462 to 64
Fax: +91-161-539472
Email: heroexports@herogroup.com

HERO CORPORATE SERVICES LIMITED
Appt. E-1, Qutab Hotel Complex
Shaheed Jeet Singh Marg
New Delhi - 110 016 INDIA
Tel.: +91-11-6850546 to 47
Fax: +91-11-6856118
Email:
general.hcs@herogrp.sprintrpg.ems.vsnl.net.in

FACT SHEET

HERO CYCLES LTD. LUDHIANA

YEAR OF START	1956
MAIN PRODUCTS / OPERATIONS	BICYCLE & BICYCLE PARTS
TOTAL TURNOVER OF GROUP	Approx. Rs. 658 crores
DOMESTIC TURNOVER	65%
FOREIGN TURNOVER	35%
CERTIFICATES	ISO 9002
STOCK EXCHANGE LISTINGS	NIL
NEW VENTURES / DIVERSIFICATION	Information Technology & Computers
MAJOR COLLABORATIONS OF HERO GROUP	• Honda Motors, Japan • Showa Manufacturing, Japan • Briggs & Stratton, USA • First Ring, USA
FLAGSHIP COMPANY	Hero Honda Motors Limited.
MAIN MARKET BEING SERVED DOMESTIC	All Over India
FOREIGN	Europe, Middle East and Africa
FAMOUS BRANDS	Cycles: Hero Ranger, Li Angel, Kidd, Piranha, Sparky, hero Miss India, Active and Hero Buzz Mopeds: Hero Majestic, Hero Puch Motor Bikes: Hero Honda, CBZ

8

Hindustan Cycle and Tube Limited

Introduction: Indian Tyre Industry

The world tyre industry is worth around US $ 70 billion. The industry is marked by the presence of around half a dozen major players, who together occupy 70% of the world market share. The worldwide tyre industry is likely to witness more restructuring after the deal between Goodyear and Sumitomo of Japan. Analysts are speculating that there will be only six to seven major players across the world after the shakeout. The big three of industry, i.e. Michelin, Bridgestone and Goodyear (before its alliance with Sumitomo), each had annual sales of US$ 12 billion. Inevitably, the alliance has increased the competitive pressure on second tier majors, notably Continental of Germany, Pirelli of Italy and Yokohama of Japan. They would also have to go on the acquisition route in order to survive. These structural developments are taking place against a backdrop of continuing overcapacity in the industry, estimated at around 30%, and slow growth in Latin America and the Asia-Pacific region in the wake of their financial crisis.

A major part of the world sales of car and truck tyres is to the replacement market. The replacement market is self-perpetuating and has inbuilt growth despite short-term setbacks from time to time. As the worldwide automotive sales are rising by a marginal 2% per annum, sales to the replacement segment will continue to dominate.

As far as Indian tyre industry is concerned, it is touching a volume of Rs. 9800 crores. In India, the growth of tyre industry depends upon the performance of the agricultural and industrial sector. While the tyre industry is mainly dominated by the organized sector, the unorganized sector holds sway in bicycle tyres. In many ways, the Indian tyre industry reflects trends in the global tyre market where capacities are concentrated in the hands of a few large players like Goodyear, Michelin, Pirelli, Bridgestone and Continental. Almost 80% of the tyre market in India is controlled by the large players leading to allegations of cartelisation in the past.

The major players in the organized tyre segment in India consist of MRF, Apollo Tyres, Ceat and JK Tyres, which account for 63% of the organized tyre market. The other key players include Modi Rubber, Kesoram Industries and Goodyear India, with 11 per cent, 7 percent and 6% share respectively. Dunlop, Falcon, Tyre Corporation of India Limited, TVS – Srichakra, Metro Tyres and Bal Krishna Tyres are some of the other players in the industry. MRF, the largest tyre manufacturer in the country, has strong brand equity. While it rules supreme in the industry, other players have created niche markets of their own.

Capacity utilization of the industry at present is 62%. Companies which have a stronger presence in the truck and bus tyres segment – Apollo, Modi, Ceat and JK enjoy higher market share in value terms, though in volume terms (measured in numbers) their share is much smaller. We may expect that the tyre industry will have more than one concern to deal with in the medium to long term. In the recent past, more than one foreign tyre major has evinced interest in entering the Indian market, which is a pointer to the fact that the industry will remain on the growth path in the near future. The tyre industry has rightly targeted at increasing the rate of radicalization in the country to cater to the changing needs of the automobile industry and the export market. The industry, in turn, expects the government to support it by legislating a favourable tariff environment. Looking ahead, a lot is needed to be done and, perhaps, the need of the hour is a concerted strategy involving both the industry and the government to face the challenges lying ahead.

The Hindustan Tyres: Profile
Background & Historical Perspective

Lala Jagjit Rai Maini, laid the foundation stone of Hindustan Tyres Ltd. in 1968 – 69. He was a lawyer with an L.L.B. degree from Lahore University. He started his business as an importer of Dunlop cycle tyres from Robinhood Cycles, Lancashire, England.

Mr. B.C. Maini, born on 10th Nov. 1944, who is now the Chairman & Managing Director of the company, joined his father, Lala Jagjit Rai Maini for business in 1968-69 just after Matriculation. Mr. Somnath Maini, younger son of Lala Jagjit Rai Maini, who is presently working as a Director of the company, is a diploma holder in rubber technology. Mr. Vijay Maini son of Mr. B.C. Maini joined his father in year 1987 – 88 after completing C.A.

In December 1968 Late Sh. Jagjit Rai Maini laid the foundation stone of Hindustan Tyre Company under Hindustan Cycle Tyres, with an initial investment of approximately Rs. 15 lacs.

In 1969-70, production of bicycle tyres and tubes started with the team effort of 150 employees at the first unit located at Industrial area-A, Ludhiana. The annual turnover was Rs. 28-29 lacs in the year 1969-70. In 1972, the second unit of Hindustan Tyres Co. started functioning at Kanganwal Road, Ludhiana.

DIVISIONS

Hindustan Tyre Co. (Unit-I)

Initial Investment of Rs. 15 Lacs (appx.)

Hindustan Tyre Co. (Unit-II)

Initial Investment of Rs. 40 Lacs (appx.)

Present Investment in both units is Rs. 700 lacs.

Relational Hierarchy of Family Members Involved in the Business

Jagjit Rai Maini

B.C. Maini

Vijay Maini

Somnath Maini

Incorporation & Integration

Hindustan Cycle and Tube Ltd. manufactures cycle tyres and tubes, and is also dealing with auto tyres and tubes. The total annual turnover of the group is Rs.140 crores, out of which exports are about Rs.7-8 crores, and domestic markets account for the remaining Rs132 crores.

The group has two units, Unit–I located at Industrial area-A, Ludhiana, and Unit–II located at Kanganwal Road Ludhiana. The present level of investment in both the units is about Rs. 700 lacs.

Sr. No	Name of the Unit	Year of start	Main product & initial investment	Location
1.	Unit No. 1	1968-69	Standard cycle tyres/tubes, Rs.15 lacs approx.	G-3, Textile Colony, Industrial Area-A, Ludhiana
2.	Unit No. 2	1972	Auto tyres & tubes & fancy tyres,	Kanganwal Road, Ludhiana

The group has 34 sale outlets in India, and is also dealing with Hero and Atlas, for supplying cycle tyres as original equipment manufacturer. The group is also exporting to countries like Egypt, South America, Turkey, Iran, Syria, etc.

The main competitors of the group are Ralson Tyres, Metro tyres and Govind Rubber. The market share of Hindustan Cycle and Tubes Ltd. is 16% in cycle tyres. The group has no stock exchange listing. It plans to start manufacturing tubeless tyres for scooters shortly.

Mission

"Faith in bright future and hence continued expansion in areas which we know the best."

Here 'continued expansion' and 'bright future' signifies

development of latest design of tyres, and to have a good R&D base so as to meet the technological or the design changes in the current business world.

Awards & Certifications

In the year 2000, the company obtained ISO 9002: 1994 certification from International Certification Ltd., New Zealand. The company received ISO - 9001 certification in May 2002.

Diversification & Expansion

YEAR	EVENT
1969	Bicycle Tyres
1972-73	ADV (auto tyres for bullock-carts etc.)
1980	Bicycle Tubes
1985-86	Diversified into auto tyres for Maruti Cars, Vans and Gypsies.
1990	Started manufacturing tyres for Tata vehicles like Tata Safari, Sumo, Sierra, Estate, and also started manufacturing auto tubes.

- The group has a team of 20 executives at unit-I and more than 30 executives at unit-II.
- The standard or the traditional cycle tyres are being manufactured in Unit-I, and fancy cycle tyres and auto tyres in Unit-II.

Raw Material Sourcing

The raw material for manufacturing tyres & tubes is being purchased from Kerala. The chemicals required for mixing in raw material for producing tyres & tubes comes from High-tech, Carbon Birla Group, Mumbai, and the carbon is sourced from Bayer, which is an American Company. The bead wire for giving strength to tyres is sourced from Tata Steel, Mumbai, and Aarti Steels, Ludhiana.

Original Equipment Manufacturer (OEM) - Status

OEM for bicycle tyres/tubes

Hero Cycles, at Ludhiana

Atlas Cycles, at Sonepat and Malanpur

OEM's purchases are of the order of about 8,000-10,000 Tyres, and 3,000-4,000 tubes per day

OEM for auto tyres/tubes

Kinetic, Pune

Hero majestic, Ludhiana

Both purchase about 10,000-20,000 tyres a day

Marketing & Distribution

- Promotion is done through advertisements in local newspapers of the potential market areas.
- Radio is also used for advertising famous brands / products of Hindustan Tyres.
- The distribution of tyres and tubes in the domestic market is done through 31 branches located in Ahmedabad, Agra, Allahabad, Ambala Cantt., Bangalore, Bareilly, Cuttak, Chandigarh, Chennai, Delhi, Guwahati, Gorakhpur, Indore, Jaipur, Kanpur, Kashipur, Kolkata, Lucknow, Ludhiana, Meerut, Muzaffarpur, Madurai, Nagpur, Patna, Pune, Ranchi, Raipur, Rohtak, Siliguri, Varanasi and Vijaywada.

The chain operates as shown below:
Company → Branch → Wholesaler → Retailer Customer

Exports

The main countries for exports are Egypt, Turkey, Iran, Syria, Dubai, Jordan, Lebanon, Peru, Argentina, Chile, and Mexico. The company has agents in these countries who distribute the products to the wholesalers or the retailers, who then distribute the product to the end consumers.

Competitors

Company's Name	**Market Share (All Over India)**
RALSON	30%
METRO	35%
GOVIND	15%
HINDUSTAN TYRES LTD.	20%

Product Portfolio

Cycle Tyres

Bicycle Tyres & Tubes

Auto Tyres & Tubes

The products have been classified as follows:
Bicycle Tyres
Agricultural Tyrès
Automobile Tyres
Two Wheeler Tyres
Tubes Valves

Sr. No.	Product	Year Of Launch	Brand	Division
1.	Standard Cycle Tyres	1968	Hindustan Tyre (HT)	Unit-I
2.	Auto Tyres	1971	Hindustan Auto Mobiles (HA)	Unit-II
3.	Auto Tyre for Three Wheeler	1972-73	Dollar	Unit -II
4.	Cycle Tubes	1980	Dhamaka	Unit – II
5.	Nylon Cycle Tyres	1986-87	Toofani Dhamaka	Unit- II
6.	Fancy Short Size Cycle Tyre	1986-87	HT	Unit - II

Brands

Bicycle Tyres

Type	Brand
A. Heavy Duty, Nylon	Bheem Arjun Mahashakti Dhamaka
B. Heavy Duty, Cotton	Black Panther Tiger Super Janta
C. Bicycle, Nylon	7 Star
D. Semi Heavy Duty	Honda Sumo Safari Punjab Mail Good Air Lucky Star Shaktimaan Raja
E. Short Size	Simta Glider Beach NDC Balloon

Cycle Tube Brands

1. Tiger
2. Arjun
3. Toofani Taqat
4. Dollar

Auto Tyre Brands

1. Plus Power
2. Rock
3. Glider
4. Rally
5. Sultan
6. Shaktimaan
7. Kissan
8. Sumo
9. Tiger
10. Panther
11. Arjun
12. Shakti
13. Commando

Face to Face with Mr. B.C. Maini Chairman and Managing Director

In the present scenario, where every company is meeting the delight of the customer by providing good quality products, whether in FMCG, electronics, durables, services, etc., Hindustan Cycles & tubes Ltd. is also in the same lane as its mission depicts, to have continued expansion by taking into account the latest development in the tyre industry.

The company is focusing on its personnel as it believes that team-work is most important in every department of the company.

The company believes that awards are not important for

them, they just want to satisfy the customer, which could be counted as the major achievement of the company. According to Mr. B.C. Maini, M.D., the success of the company can be attributed to Marketing Department because it is this department which exploits the weaknesses of the competitors and produce quality and durable products.

Mr. Maini believes that HRM is an important functional area. As the capabilities of the management and senior officials are reflected in the company's working environment, HRM plays a very crucial role for the group.

The company proposes to set up a new unit for manufacturing Radial Auto Tyres in the near future. The view of the MD was that the cycle trade is low paid, and burden of export of the cycle tyre is on India so the production reserved for export will increase to 20% in future.

The competitive strength of the company lies in the economies of scale, and well-equipped R&D. The unit is being run with minimum of overheads and has the lowest interest burden in the whole tyre industry. The main competitive advantage for exports is the lower labour cost as compared to any other country. Even in China and Argentina, the labour cost is about $20 day. In India the major competitive weakness in any business is that long commitment is not possible as policies change very frequently.

The markets with high potential in India are of U.P., Madurai and Chennai, whereas in exports, Egypt (according to volume), and Latin America and Europe (according to profits), offer the greatest potential. Turnover of cycle tyres/tubes is Rs.120 crores, and of auto tyres/tubes is about Rs.20 crores.

The complete range of bicycle and auto tyres/tubes is

available with Hindustan Tyre Company. The cost of production, according to the company is less and there are two shifts of twelve hours each. Rejection rate is also very low.

The Indian market is very large and is still not saturated, so it offers prospects for growth for every company. Developed countries have stopped manufacturing cycle tyres /tubes. Hence, India has the opportunity to export in bulk to such countries. Now export markets can be explored more thoroughly through web sites, which was not possible 20 years ago.

Information technology is playing a major role now. One can locate customers in half an hour without any wastage of resources.

Hindustan Tyres Ltd. fulfills its social responsibility by offering ample opportunities for employment of young managers. Secondly, it provides for a pollution-free environment by utilising new devices or technologies.

Management education, today, should lay stress on all-round development of students, not only in academics but also in other fields.

The cycle industry is growing and the future of Hindustan Tyres & Tubes is bright.

Data Sheet

Year Of Start	1968-69
Main Products/Operations	Auto Tyres/Tubes, Cycle Tyres/Tubes
Total Turnover	Rs.140 Crores
Domestic Turnover	Rs.130-132 Crores
Export Turnover	Rs.7-8 Crores
Percentage Of Different Products In Turnovers	Bicycles tyres and tubes – about 80% Auto tyres and tubes – about 20%
Certificates	ISI and ISO 9002
Stock Exchange Listing	Nil
New Ventures / Future Plans	After 6-7 Years To Have A Venture With Any Foreign Radial Tyre Manufacturing Company
Flagship Co.	Hindustan Cycles And Tubes Ltd.
Main Domestic Market	All Over India
Main Export Markets	Egypt, South America, Iran, Syria Etc.

Name and Designation of Main Employees:

Sr. No.	NAME	DESIGNATION
1.	Sh. Parshottam Narula	Sr. Sales Manager
2.	Sh. Shamsher Singh	Manager Marketing
3.	Sh. Satish Bakshi	Area Manager
4.	Sh. R.S. Walia	Area Manager
5.	M.M. Chopra	Personnel Manager
6.	Sh. S.K. Mehta	Works Manager
7.	Sh. Anil Jalota	Manager Accounts
8.	Sh. Arun Mishra	Production Manager, Unit-I
9.	Sh. J.N. Mishra	Production Manager, Unit-II
10.	Sh. T.C. Sharma	Production Manager, Auto
11.	Sh. Parveen Maini	Production Manager, Tubes

9

Malwa Group of Companies

Introduction: Indian Textile Industry

Structure of the Industry

The Indian textile Industry has a complex structure. On one hand it is marked by the presence of large-scale organised players, and on the other hand are the numerous small scale independent units.

The growth of the small-scale independent unit was backed by middlemen in the textile fabric trade. Traditionally textiles have had a long chain for distribution with various intermediaries like Wholesalers, Distributors, Agents, etc. These intermediaries were the marketing arms of mills and played a major role in maintaining contact with the final customer, the retailer. The mills, being manufacturing oriented, lost all contact with the final customer and, as a result the intermediary became all-powerful. The intermediaries, in order to sustain their businesses resorted to buying from independent units.

The growth of garment exports from India, led to a demand for 'made to order' fabrics. Thus, the garment exporters/middlemen started approaching these independent units with their own designs. Doing business with the independent units gave the garment manufacturer a higher degree of flexibility.

Fragmentation in the textile industry, per se, is not bad. It has positives attached to it like keeping a check on price increases, possibilities of running smaller lots, etc. However, the negatives far outweigh the positives in the Indian context. Small size does not permit economies of scale and thus reduces the absolute margin available that could have been used for technological advancement, research and development, and brand building.

Some Highlights

- The Indian textile industry is one of the largest segments of the Indian economy accounting for over one-fifth of the total industrial production
- The industry has a complex structure marked by presence of large scale production units as well as small scale independent units
- The industry is manufacturer driven with spinning having large scale operations and the retailing as the weakest link

The Spinning Industry

- India is the third largest producer of cotton in the world and also has a strong production base for synthetic fibres
- The Indian spinning industry is dominated by cotton yarn which also accounts for 80% of total value of yarn exports
- With an installed capacity of 37 Mn. spindles, India accounts for about 20% of the world's spindle capacity

The Weaving and Knitting Industry

- The fabric production industry can be divided into 3 sectors viz. Powerloom, handloom and mill sector
- The decentralised sector accounts for 95% of the total cloth production
- Knitted fabric forms 18% of the total fabric production
- Despite the largest loomage in the world, India's share in shuttle-less looms is only 1.35 %

The Indian Fabric Processing Industry

- Processing is the weakest link in India's entire textile chain
- The processing industry is decentralised and is marked by hand processing units, independent units, and the composite mill sector
- Indian fabric processing industry has deployed low·end technology with little investment initiative in technology upgradation
- The Indian processing industry lacks R&D and innovation

The Garment Manufacturing Sector

- The apparel industry is the largest foreign exchange earner accounting for 12% of India's exports
- Small scale fabricators dominate the garment manufacturing sector
- Most of the manufacturing units are medium technology level

The Malwa Group: A Profile

Background/Historical Perspective

The Oswal family is known for its magnificent contribution towards textile industry of India. The family splits resulted into the generation of different group as listed below:

Malwa Group	Vidya Sagar Oswal & Jangi Lal Oswal
Nahar Group	Vidya Sagar Oswal & Jawahar Lal Oswal
Vardhman	Rattan Chand & S.P. Oswal
Oswal Spinning	Lachman Das Oswal & Ashok Oswal
Shreyans	Rattan Chand & D.K. Oswal

If there is one thing that distinguishes the Oswals from the country's other business families, it is only 'gut – feel'.

This has kept them afloat even after six successive splits. 85 years ago, an 11-year-old boy left his village in search of livelihood. Over a period of time he created a business empire of over Rs.2000 crores. Lala Vidya Sagar Oswal (96) was studying in the 4th standard when he lost his father to plague, which had spread in the area at that time. He was the eldest son in the family. He decided to move out to Ludhiana.

There he started an arthiya shop and then a provisions store. However, he suffered losses in both ventures. Ultimately he took up a job on a monthly salary of Rs. 10 with Faqir Chand, a leading hosiery manufacturer of his time, with an assurance that he would be allowed to learn the technicalities of the job. The entrepreneur in him was always alive and vibrant and he picked up the nuances of the trade. His mother helped him by selling all her jewellery. He installed a machine and started manufacturing socks. The business kept on growing, and in a span of a few years he installed 10 more machines.

Family Tree

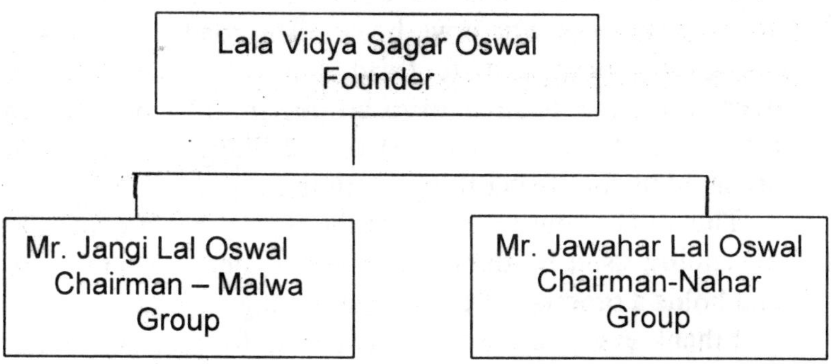

Message from the Founder

Lala Vidya Sagar Oswal

As founder of VSO Group, I feel a strong sense of pride and honour to head such an exceptional organization. Exceptional in every regard, be it dedication to work, a sense of commitment to the customer or maintaining quality standards. Most of all, in winning over customers confidence which to us is the prime reason for our success day after day, year after year.

Achievement brings with it a sense of pride which further encourages the growth of the people, the company and the product line. As we look back over the years, we have come a long way from where we began. The road to success has not always been easy to tread, but each hurdle that we overcame gave us strength to go one more step ahead. We took each challenge as a part of the bigger process which prepared us for greater things in time to come.

The VSO Group, a vision of the future that is continually expanding itself by the basic qualities, necessary to growth and holds a promise of even greater things to come.

I thank every one at the VSO Group for their unwavering faith and conviction which has made it possible for the vision to come true. It is my distinct privilege to share it with you.

Incorporation and Integration: Lala Vidya Sagar Oswal Group

The VSO Group is committed to its belief in the basics. From its humble beginning, way back in 1931, to today, the Group has always engaged in industrial activities that cater to the basic necessities of life, knit wears, cotton, yarn, vegetable oils, vanaspati, sugar, paper & Denim.

This commitment is also reflected in future ventures in agro-based industries and the infrastructure sector.

Group Companies

- Malwa Cotton Spinning
- Punjab Wool combers Ltd
- Malwa Industries Ltd
- Oswal Knit India
- Mukerian paper Mills
- Oswal Sugars Ltd.

Malwa Cotton Spinning

Popularly called Malwa is among the top ten textile mills of the Indian sub continent. The total spindleage of the two units is around 1,40,000. The first unit was incorporated in the year 1976 in Barnala, District Sangrur, in the state of Punjab. And the second came into being in the year 1988 at Paonta Sahib, District Sirmour, in the state of Himachal Pradesh.

Headed by Shri Jangi Lal Oswal, Chairman cum Managing Director, Malwa Cotton Spinning Mills Ltd. has benefited greatly under his expert supervision and valuable experience. He has pumped new life into the industry by supplementing the units with very efficient machinery which proved to be not only economically viable but also improved on quality and range of yarn being produced.

The mills are equipped with hitech state of art machineries from world renowned textile machinery manufacturers like Reiter, Trutzler, Crossrol, Schloforst and Savio. The above process machines are also equipped with latest on line quality control equipments combined with computerised information system. World wide recognised and accepted high reliability Uster quality control equipments form the core of company's R&D and constant monitoring quality control department. An extremely dedicated, skilful work-force of 5000 workers, including highly experienced textile professionals, is the driving force that ultimately yields products that are unique. In-house training keeps the staff updated with technologies abroad. The team, headed by dynamic chairman, Mr. Jangi Lal Oswal is committed to meet the challenges of Global textile exacting standards. Malwa Yarn is sought by domestic & international markets. The products are widely demanded the world over.

Punjab Woolcombers Ltd

Envisaging a vast potential in wool, Punjab Woolcombers Ltd. was conceived and incorporated in the year 1977. It rapidly grew to become India's finest wool combing unit and the largest manufacturer of 'Wool Mark' woollen worsted hosiery yarn. Set over sprawling 9.25 acre plot in the business centre of Ludhiana in the State of Punjab, it has grown from strength to strength to boast of the finest equipment, technology and skilled personnel that are on the job to produce high quality wool , symbolic of Punjab Woolcombers Ltd.

At the plant, wool combing, dyeing of fibres/yarns, worsted spinning, woollen spinning and manufacturing of other textile goods is carried out.

About 3 million pounds of combed wool is produced here annually. State - of the - art equipment hums at the plant, heralding quality standards which have found recognition of world class wool by the International Wool Secretariat (IWS) for its woollen worsted yarn and also recognised by the Australian Wool Corporation.

Diversification and expansion has led to the setting up of a project to manufacture Fine Lambs wool Yarn. A new wool spinning unit has been established for this particular purpose. Constantly on the lookout for changes, the Research teams are guiding the company in to the future. Readiness to adapt and accommodate changes has been the building block around which technology has triumphed and ensured that only the finest wool is produced and delivered to the customer. Consistency is the key which has kept Punjab Woolcombers Ltd. growing and made it possible for it to achieve many distinction. With an attitude that balances technology, precision and quality control, Punjab Woolcombers Limited is set to chart a success that is as different and determined as The VSO Group.

Malwa Industries Ltd

This is a part of Malwa Group , based in Northern India

with sales offices all over India and overseas, Malwa Industries excel in the field of spinning high quality multi-variety of cotton and synthetic yarn and also manufactures world class Sweaters under the brand name Casablanca and is licensee of " Pringle of Scotland".

The Denim plant is strategically located close to the heart of the finest cotton growing areas of Northern India. The plant is fully integrated with State-of-the-Art machinery from Switzerland, USA, Belgium and Japan to give its customers the Real Classical Indigo Denim, made with the best Rope Dyed Technology under an Eco-Friendly Environment. With the aim to meet both the physical and visual standards, the company has the flexibility to meet the trends in all aspect of design, appearance and other developments which is expected by today's fashion conscious market.

The machinery and the facilities are equally complemented with highly motivated and skilled workforce which works round the clock to deliver a world-class product. The aim is to produce variants of Denim in number of weights, widths and roll lengths as desired by the customers. The target is to suit the needs of every Garments Manufacturer, large or small, to give the optimum levels in performance from cutting room to customer satisfaction.

To ensure the optimum performance in garment manufacturing and to reduce cost and reach the best fabric utilisation levels, the company tries to give its customers a fabric which has undergone rigorous Internationally recognised System of Quality Assurance at each stage of production. Thereby reducing:

- Wastage
- Rejection

Plant and Equipment: Malwa Cotton

The production capacity of the Barnala unit is 30 tonnes per day and the Paonta Sahib unit spins out 38 tonnnes per day. The product is versatile and finds use in many different ways in the textile and clothing industry of which it forms the essential ingredient.

Spinning out from the unit is a wide range of yarns made from Cotton, Acrylic, Polyester, Viscose and other synthetic fibres, Cotton yarn produced is both carded and combed, then there is Acrylic yarn, polyester Viscose yarn and other blends in dyed and Grey.

The high quality of the product has carved a place for itself in the export market where all kinds of cotton yarns, synthetic yarns and their blends are exported. Export growths have been phenomenal and predict the future trends. Malwa Cotton Spinning Mills Ltd. has been marked from the beginning to spin a success story of its own.

The experienced cotton selectors of the company are

spread across the cotton belt of Punjab. Control on quality of Cotton is exercised to keep it contamination free right from picking stage.

Cotton is ginned in the company's modern Ginning Unit comprising of both Saw and Roller Gin. Each bale passes out of Ginning Factory only after it meets Malwa's Quality Standards. The contamination free bales produced in the Ginning Factory meet Uster HVI900 Grade. Cotton is processed in mills of the company under controlled conditions created by sophisticated state-of-art, Humidity and Textile Air Engineering System provided by Luwa Humidification System. Each process confirms to stringent quality norms specified by Textile Research Association of India.

Quality: Malwa Cotton

Quality of the product is constantly monitored at various stages of yarn manufacturing. Savio winders of the company are equipped with third generation contamination control Uster cleaners & coupled with Air Splicers

ESPERO VOLUFIL CONE TO CONE BULKING:

First time in India, the Company has imported world class cone to cone bulking (continuos shrinking and bulking) and winding machine VOLUFIL, model ESPERO from Savio, Italy, for shrinking of acrylic yarn, Hb and blends, and wool and blend set yarn. The Machine is derived from the latest technological development of contiums shrinking system, which ensures complete shrinking through out the yarn which acquires an extremely regular structure and shows excellent volume and roundness. This machine is equipped with electronic yarn clears and mobile splicer. The packages produced by this machine have optimal density metering and uniformity.

A 66KV sub-station in the plant backed by own diesel generation sets, assures continuous power supply and hence continuos production at the plant.

Wearing a light cotton shirt, a snug sweatshirt or a soft lambs wool sweater gives an individual a feeling of physical well being. Such comfort depends essentially on the quality of yarn used. The units of Malwa Cotton, with its spreaded wings Oswal Knit India, Malwa Processing House and Punjab Woolcombers Ltd. are equipped with the most sophisticated third generation equipments of Zellweger Uster, the world market leader in textile electronics which enables Malwa industry to manufacture optimum quality and competitive products from fiber to yarn. The company has all the testing and monitoring systems used in raw material inspection, in process production phases, and final yarn.

Customer Support

The customer Service cell of Malwa Industries endeavours to answer all the questions of the customers, solve their problems, and respond to all their queries, to maximum possible extent. A team of highly experienced technologists can give a full back up to all areas of fabric processing, particularly in garment finishing treatments. The customer can be helped to choose the right fabric for a particular garment so that all his expectations in the areas of comfort, design and fashion are fully met with. Effort is made to deliver value to the product.

The team is available 24 hours a day to help customers face the challenges of today's ever-changing fashion industry.

Raw Material

Dedicated, committed and involved cotton selectors of the company at different stations, headed by experienced supervisors, and Vice President, spares no pain in the selection of Kapas or Raw cotton available in the market. Kapas is ginned in company's own well-established saw and roller ginning factory at Fazilka.

Before ginning, utmost care is taken to weed out all foreign matters like jute thread, coloured polypropylene foils, contaminated fiber, turfs, pieces of coloured threads and fabrics, ropes, feathers etc, by experienced workers. Selected samples of individual lots are further tested at HVI 900 Spin Lab System. On the basis of quality characteristics, the better graded lots are given green signal for procurement. Ginned lots are once again tested and graded at the works for the various characteristics and put into designated godowns. Before taking into mix and finally feeding into blow-room line, each and every bale of different type is opened and sorted out for all remaining foreign matters by functionally and actively well trained competent manpower to get the very best quality of yarn.

It is company's aim to match the quality of yarn and services to the requirement of its customers. The Company has developed its reputation owing to its efforts to supply desired quality and timely delivery of yarn to both domestic and international customers, Constant upgradation of the quality of yarn is also being carried out.

Awards and Certifications

In recognition of the company's export performance; Govt. of India awarded the status of "Export House", an award conferred to selective textile mills. Malwa conform to ISO 9002 standards in production.

Thus, knotless, flawless & high quality yarn confirming to Uster standards is produced. Acrylic fiber is procured from world-renowned manufacturers and Acrylic cotton yarn & high bulk Acrylic yarn are produced. Dye house facility at company's works enables it to produce dyed yarn of exact shades.

Malwa Cotton also produces polyester yarn, polyester cotton yarn, viscose yarn, dyed viscose yarn and viscose cotton yarn. Raw materials like polyester, viscose are procured from reputed manufacturers.

Malwa Cotton has bagged ISO 9002 certification the highest mark of recognition on the international scale. This is an achievement not by accident but as a result of constant endeavour and commitment to all round excellence and total customers satisfaction both in India and Overseas.

Products/Services: Malwa Cotton

1,40,000 spindles spread over Punjab and Himachal Pradesh give a production of

Cotton Yarn	:	45 tonnes/day
Acrylic Yarn	:	25 tonnes/day
Polyester Viscose Yarn	:	10 tonnes/day

Description of Products

- 100% Cotton Yarn (All Counts NE)
- Acrylic / Cotton Yarn (Count NE, in any Blend Ratio)
- Polyester Cotton Yarn In any Blend Ratio
- Cotton Viscose
- 100% Acrylic (All counts in NM)
- Polyester/ Viscose, 100% Polyester, 100% Polyester
- Viscose

Product Range of the Company: Punjab Woolcombers

100% Pure Wool	Woolmark
	For Hosiery
60% Pure Wool 40% Acrylic	For Hosiery
100% Acrylic	For Hosiery
100% Acrylic	For Hosiery For Weaving
70% Polyester 30% Wool	For Weaving
Lambs Wool Yarn 90:10 Wool : Nylon	For Hosiery
Shetland Yarn 70:30, Wool:Nylon	For Hosiery

Product Range: Malwa Industries

1. Basic OE x OE Indigo "Casablanca"
2. Basic Ring "Pringle"
3. Lycra Stretch "Body Wrap"
4. Indigo Cords "Magical Moods"
5. Silky Chino " Comforts"
6. Coloured Weft "Deadly Duo"

Foreign Presence: Malwa Cotton

The company is engaged in exports of all kind of yarn for the last 7 Years. Products are well accepted in Asia, Europe, Africa & American continents.

World-wide export markets include:

Asian-Market	European Market	African Market
Japan	Germany	South Africa
China	U.K.	Egypt
Korea	Russia	Kenya
U.A.E.	Spain	Mauritius
Hong Kong	Italy	Nigeria
Singapore	Switzerland	Sudan
Cyprus	Belgium	Tanzania
Israel	Cuba	
Malaysia	Greece	
Taiwan	Portugal	
Turkey	Slovenia	
Vietnam	Sweden	
Bangladesh		

Malwa Cotton Spinning Mills handles design, production, marketing and sales at Ludhiana, and yarn manufacturing at Barnala (Punjab) and Paonta Sahib (H.P.).

Market and International Operations:
Punjab Woolcombers
Punjab Woolcombers is currently exporting to the following countries: Dubai, Saudi Arabia, Pakistan, Kenya, Algeria, Canada, Tanzania, Mauritius, Nepal And Bangladesh

Contact Information: Malwa Cotton
Registered and Head Office:
Malwa Cotton Spinning Mills Ltd.
Industrial Area 'A',
Ludhiana-141003, (Pb.)India
Phones (91-161) 2644201
Fax : 91-161 - 2662240, 2669619
Telex : 81 386-467 E-mail : ho.malwa@vsogroup.com

U.K. Office:
Malwa Cotton Spinning Mills Ltd.
9, Severn Road, Oadby,
Leicester-LE2 4FU
UNITED KINGDOM
Phone : 0044 116 271 6894
Fax : 0044 116 271 6060
E-Mail : malwa@globalnet.co.uk

Mumbai Office:
Malwa Cotton Spinning Mills Ltd.
708-709, Raheja Chambers,
213, Nariman Point,
MUMBAI-400 021.
Phone: 91-22-22027322, 22843217, 22854070, 22854083
Fax: 91-22-22874847

Delhi Corporate Office:
Malwa Cotton Spinning Mills Ltd.
DCM Building,
2R, II Floor,
16, Barakhamba Road,
New Delhi - 110 001
Phone: 91-11-23719133, 23755159, 23715959
Fax: 91-11-23755169

Works: Barnala Unit
Malwa Cotton Spinning Mills Ltd.
Village Harigarh,
Raikot Road,
Barnala
Tel: 91-1679-20262,20907
Fax: 91-1679-32365

Works: Paonta Sahib Unit
Malwa Cotton Spinning Mills Ltd.
Village Patlian,
Paonta Sahib (HP)
Tel: 91-1704-22255,22455
Fax: 91-1704-22690

Contact Address of the Company: Punjab Woolcombers

Regd. Office & Works:

Dhandari Kalan,
G.T. Road,
Ludhiana-141 010
Tel: 91-161-2672900,2670198,2672199,2672434
Fax: 91-161-2672197, 2672436
Email : info.pwc@vsogroup.com
Spinning Unit:
Village Mangarh
(Kohara)
Ludhiana

10

Metro Tyres Limited

Introduction: Indian Tyre Industry

The last decade of the twentieth century witnessed an immense transformation of business systems globally – from tightly regulated markets to deregulated market, from centralised, authoritarian control to more horizontal systems, from a monopoly of decision making by a few to more widespread participation by widening circles of employees, from labour intensive companies to greater reliance on computerised work processes, from isolated domestic markets to trans-continental ones, from a narrow technical concept of business to one in which people and society are encompassed.

The Indian tyre industry is a Rs.9800 crore industry. There is a daily traffic of over 4.12 lakh trucks, 1.27 lakh buses, 7.23 lakh cars, and thousands of taxis, two-wheelers, three-wheelers, tractors and animal drawn vehicles on the roads. There exists a vast potential for the tyre industry in India. The fortune of this industry depends on the agricultural and industrial performance of the economy, the transportation needs, and the production of vehicles. In the last 5 years, this industry managed to achieve a compounded annual growth of barely 4.40 percent. Well known brands like Pirelli's, Kumho, Falken, Yokohoma, Continental and Michelline are making their presence felt in the country and gaining ground on account of greater durability, superior finish, extended warranty period for manufacturing defects, and better service facilities. Imported tyre brands come with a better warranty and are better than Indian tyres in terms of technology and services.

Presently around 50,000 tyres are imported in the country annually. Indian tyre industry is in urgent need of technological upgradation, more so the small and medium companies. The process of liberalisation is now irreversible. Industry will have to face international competition in terms of free imports of technologically superior products at very competitive prices. R & D is the key to technological changes, but this is one area where Indian tyre industry has to do a lot of catching up with its global competitors. A quantum jump in productivity is a must for survival and could be achieved through training of human resources and improved manufacturing techniques.

The industry would be able to survive only by producing goods comparable with the best in the world and at competitive prices. This is possible only through judicious deployment of materials, manufacturing processes and value engineering. Most of India's tyre majors like J.K. Tyres, Ceat, MRF and Apollo, have put up exclusive showrooms – the kinds one would associate with upmarket garment stores – across the country and this new trend is going to stay.

Metro Tyres Ltd.: A Profile

Background and Historical Perspective

Sardar Mann Singh, 74 yrs old, started his career in trading of tyres and tubes at Kanpur in the sixties. In 1967-68 he got the idea to become an entrepreneur, as at that time there was acute shortage of tyres & tubes in the market. At that time tyres & tubes were sold at ration depots. Sardar Mann Singh took it as an opportunity and started manufacturing tyres & tubes.

Mr. Rummy Chabra, 40, and Mr. Navneet Chabra, 35, Sons of Sardar Mann Singh are both graduates and married. Both of them are deeply involved in the family business and are making concrete efforts to make their business grow in the face of general recession that is being faced by this industry.

Family Tree

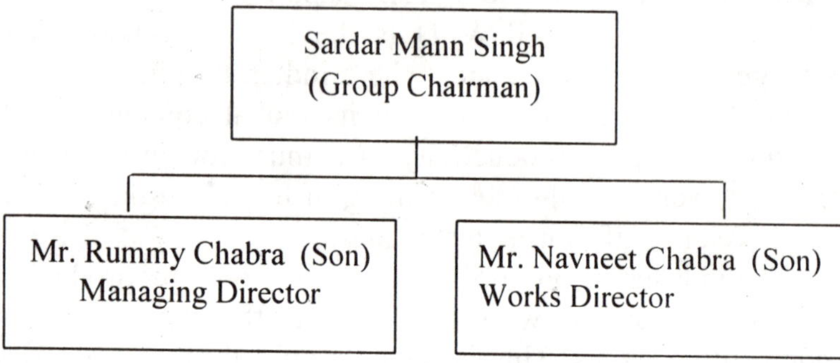

Incorporation and Integration

From a humble beginning in 1968, with 20-25 employees, and a turnover of Rs. 20-50 lacs, Metro Tyres made steady progress to establish itself as a market leader for bicycle tyres & tubes in India and achieved a turnover of Rs 300 crores. As a result of steady increase in production of quality products, the company ventured overseas and developed a niche for itself in the international market as well. The company also kept itself abreast with latest technologies and developed Nylon tyres and Butyl tubes through its own R & D efforts.

MTL was incorporated on 18/1/1974 under the Indian Companies Act, 1956, as a private limited company with the main object to manufacture cycle tyres & tubes, and pioneered the shift of the cycle tyre industry to the northern part of the country. Today this industry has flourished to such an extent that more than 70% of the total demand of cycle tyres and tubes of the country is met by manufacturers based in Ludhiana. The company is being effectively managed since inception and has always stressed on stringent quality standards. The products are well accepted in the national as well as international markets.

Metro's most precious asset is its professionally trained and dedicated human resource. Ludhiana is one of the main centres for manufacturing bicycles. In the year 1980, MTL diversified & took up the manufacture of bicycle and auto chains. Presently it is one of the leading manufacturer of these parts.

MTL has four units in Ludhiana

Unit 1: 503, Industrial Area B, Ludhiana.
Unit 2: B-27, Focal Point, Ludhiana.
Unit 3: Jugiana, GT Road, Ludhiana.
Unit 4: B-46, Focal Point, Ludhiana.

In the year 1983, the company diversified into the manufacture of tyres & tubes for scooters, motor cycles, LCVs, Animal Driven Vehicles and Tractors, under the brand name of '**Metro**'. These products have also been well accepted in the market.

In the year 1999, an off-take agreement was signed with Continental AG, Germany, for the manufacture of bicycle tyres & tubes under the '**Continental**' brand. To implement this project, an ultra modern plant with state-of-the-art machinery was set up. This plant employs the latest technology for the manufacture of bicycle tyres & tubes.

Quality Policy of the Group

We (Metro Tyres Ltd.) will strive to achieve prosperity & customer satisfaction through continuous improvement in the product quality, competitive pricing and timely delivery.

Quality Objectives of the Group

1. Upgrading product processes and technology.
2. Training employees to achieve continuous improvement in their work areas.
3. Building and improving quality through process control.
4. Increasing production capacity to achieve the targets.

Diversification and Expansion

The company has diversified into the field of home appliances such as electric fans, electric irons, sewing machines, etc, under the brand name "**ORTEM**". Keeping the customer foremost in mind and for the convenience of buyers, the company established a full-fledged "Export Division" at New Delhi. The export division has the capability for entertaining & servicing enquiries relating not only to the company products, but also for non-company commodities and engineering goods.

Metro Appliances Limited

ORTEM – Brand Ceiling Fans are being manufactured at Noida. This unit is being managed by Rummy Chabra.

Awards and Certifications

Metro Tyres & Tubes and home appliances of the company have also been granted 'ISI' certification by the Bureau of Indian Standards. Incidentally, it was the first company in industry to achieve this distinction.

PRODUCTS/SERVICES

Bicycle Division

Tyres

Tubes

Chains

Auto Division

Tyres for

Mopeds

Motor Cycles

Scooters

Three Wheelers

Hand Carts

Jeeps

Tractors

S. No.	Product	Branch	Launch	Unit
1.	Cycle Tyres	Metro	1968	503, Industrial Area B- Ludhiana
2.	Cycle Tubes	Metro	1970	503, Industrial Area B- Ludhiana
3.	Bicycle nylon/cotton tyres	Metro	1987	503, Industrial Area B- Ludhiana
4.	Cycle chains	Metro	1983	503, Industrial Area B- Ludhiana

Cycle Tyres

Bicycle tyres are made from natural as well as synthetic rubber & are of two types: cotton & nylon.

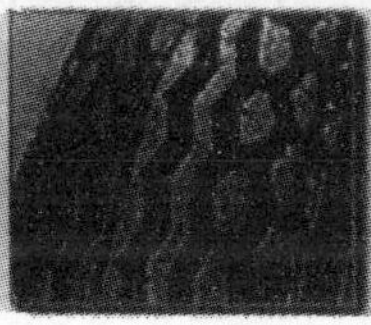

Cycle Tubes

Bicycle tubes are moulded from either of the following materials:

Natural rubber or Butyl rubber

Bicycle Chains

Bicycle chains can be supplied in any number of links or in rolls of 150 meters. Each chain is packed in a Metro box, and 50 boxes are packed in a master carton. A 150 meters chain, wound on a metal spool, is packed in a strong wooden case.

Tyres for Auto Segment

Moped, Motorcycle, Scooter, Three Wheelers, Hand Carts

Jeep **Tractors**

Ortem Fans, New Delhi

Company Name: Metro Appliances Ltd.

Located at: New Delhi

Standard: ISO 9002:1994

Scope of Registration: Manufacture & Supply of Tested Fans.

Rummy Chabra, S/o Sardar Mann Singh, handles the unit.

 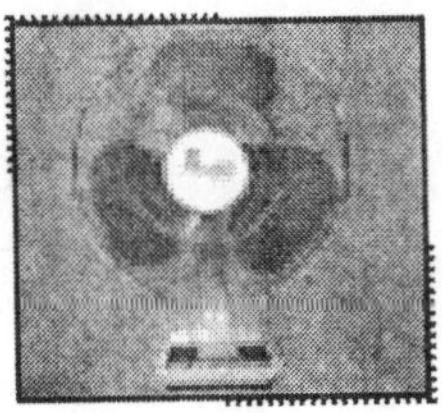 

Data Sheet

Company Name	MTL
Started In	1968
Current no. of employees	4500
Products	Bicycle tyres & tubes, bicycle chains, automobile tyres & tubes
Export Destinations	Germany, Europe, Middle East
Buy Back Arrangement	AG Continental Germany
Sales Offices	76 throughout India in the name of Metro Sales. Dealer network of 15000 all over India.
Total turnover	Rs 300 crores
Export Turnover	15% of total turnover
Domestic Turnover	85% of total turnover
Growth	Stagnant because of recession
Exhibitions attended	Successful participation in prestigious exhibition like IFMA, Germany

Organisation Chart

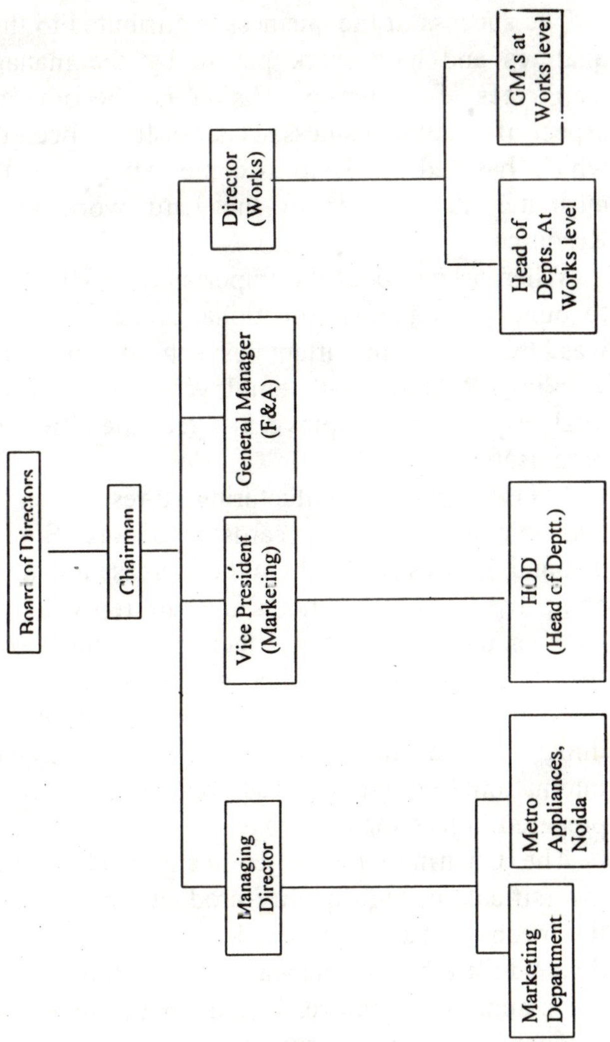

Face to Face with Mr G S Dhiman
G M Marketing

The success of the business is attributed to the leadership qualities and hard work put in by the management and employees of the group. 'Vision' has become an important aspect of today's business scenario. It has been the 'Vision', which has led MTL to become what it is today. MTL attributes its success to the hard work of its Human Resource.

When asked about the importance of HRM as compared to other management functional areas, he said that HRM was the most important aspect of any organisation's working. Relation with employees had become the most vital aspect, as employees were the lifeblood of any organisation.

MTL started manufacturing tyres when tyres were available against ration cards at depots. Since 1968, the demand of tyres has been on the increase and the sales of the company have been increasing. In reply to the question whether the company was facing any threat from foreign firms, especially from China, Mr. Dhiman said that presently Ludhiana industry was facing recession but hoped that things would improve. As far as competition from international companies was concerned, he said they were prepared to face the challenge.

The Chairman of the company was of the view that diversification, high quality product, and collaborations are the means to tackle the challenges of globalisation. Today, demand for the products was less as compared to the supply, the company, therefore, had no plans for expansion. The company was only channelling its efforts to maintain its present level of business.

Talking about the benefits the company had derived from

IT, he said that introduction of IT had provided a lot of benefits. Timely generation of reports, easy information transformation, global access to information, etc, were the benefits of using IT. When asked how the company was trying to fulfil its social responsibility, he said that they were standing where they needed to stand for social welfare.

Talking about the strengths and weaknesses of the group, he said that Quality, Brand, CRM, Supply Chain Management and Zero Defects were the main strengths of the company.

When asked about the role played by management institutes in providing good managers to the industry, he remarked that the number of management institutes was high but quality education was nowhere to be seen. Government should take care of this aspect. Management students should be given adequate opportunity to have practical orientation to theoretical concepts. To this end the industry should assist the management institutes.

When asked about the future plans of the company, the Chairman said that the group was constantly making efforts to grow. Let us see where the wind blows.

11

Nahar Group of Companies

Introduction: Indian Textile Industry

Textile industry is one of the oldest industries existing today. Initially this industry catered to the basic need to cover the human body. Historically, mankind has relied on natural fibers, cotton, wool and silk for it's textile products. At that time, the technology for manufacture of fabric was relatively simple. However, today this industry has assumed a totally enhanced dimensions.

During the initial years of its existence, woolen industry mostly catered to the requirement of the armed forces. Woolen manufacture in the organized form started in 1876 when the first mechanized woolen mill was set up at Kanpur. The industry progressed rather slowly, till 1947, after which it leaped forward. Today, this industry has achieved progress in all directions, including sizable export earnings. In 1950,there were only 16 units in the organized sector operating in the country. Today, there are as many as 658 registered units. The installed capacity of the industry has increased enormously during the last 50 years or so.

The Industrial revolution was the turning point for the textile industry. Earlier, goods were manufactured by hand, but after the industrial revolution, machines substituted men and production started on a large scale. After independence, textile industry in India began to grow, but it was only after the "New Economic Policy of 1991" that the Textile industry really started growing. As a result of liberalisation, Globalisation and Privatisation the textile industry has touched an all time high in production.

Sector	Degree of Integration	Technology Level	Scale
SSI Spinning	Only Spinning	Hand spinning	Cottage Industry
Non- SSI Spinning	Only Spinning	Ring/ Rotor Spinning	15,000 spindles or 800 rotors
Handloom Sector	Only Weaving	Weaving by Handlooms	Cottage Industry
Powerloom Sector	Only Weaving	Primarily shuttle-less looms	Conventional units: 4-8 looms; Moder Units: 25 looms
Mills	Spinning & Weaving	Ring/ Rotor Spinning Primarily shuttle-less looms	15,000 spindles or 800 rotors and 50 looms
Knitting Units	Only Knitting	Modern Machinery	NA
Hand Processors (woven fabrics)	Only processing	Hand processing with out the use of Power	Upto 5000 mtrs per day
Indepen-dent Process Houses (IPH)	Only processing	Primarily Batch dyeing	20,000 mtrs fabric per day
Composite Mills	Spinning, Weaving & processing	Ring/Rotor Spinning, Shuttle-less Looms, Continuos dyeing	20,000 to 40,000 mtrs of Finished fabric per day
Garment manufac-turers	Only Garment Manufacturing	Basic Machines with few Work aids	25 sewing machines

Indian wool is mainly suitable for the manufacture of carpets. For Apparel Grade wool, we have to rely on imports from Australia. In 1964, the government set up the Export Promotion Council. As a result of this, the exports of woollen products have increased from 31 million US$ in 1964-65 to 470 million US$ in 1996-97. The export earnings in 1964-65 were mainly from raw wool and woollen carpets. In 1996-97, value added products including woollen/acrylic knitwear, woollen woven readymade garments, worsted fabrics, yarn and shawls/scarves, have contributed significantly to export earnings.

Today the industry structure is fragmented with certain sectors such a spinning being strong and areas like processing being weaker and acting as bottlenecks to the industry's development.

The industry being manufacturer driven, has the largest scale of operations in the Spinning sector and retailing being a lean link.

The industry is characterised by the following players:

- **Cotton Farm and Ginning Sector:** A highly fragmented set of operators with very low infusion of technology in their systems. This is probably one of the reasons for the low yield levels of Indian cotton.
- **Synthetic & Man-made Fibre/Filament Industry:** A capital intensive sector dominated by very few players under pressure from Stagnating demand and cheaper imports coming from the Far-East. While India is regarded largely as a Cotton player in the International market, the sector needs to grow and project a multi-fibre face. One reason for that has been the lack of developments in the processing industry of India that has not kept pace with the international advancements in processing technology, majority of which has happened

in the Manmade and Synthetic Industry. Thus India is still not regarded a good producer of Tencel, Lycra, light weight Micro-filament fabrics, Polynosics, etc.

- **Spinning Sector:** A sector boosted in the early 90s decade by surge in exports. This period also noticed the entry of many new players into the industry. This sector is more advanced in terms of machinery in compared to the overall Textile Industry. Owing to a number of players present, however still not as fragmented as the weaving, processing and the garmenting sectors of the industry (because of high capital costs in these projects), spinning in India is witnessing a serious domestic over capacity and is under price pressure.
- **Weaving Sector:** The fragmented Powerloom and Handloom sectors account for about 95% of weaving in India. Powerlooms have thrived vis-à-vis the mills given the cost structure they operate under. The Powerloom sector has taken advantage of the low labour cost, tax and fiscal benefits, however the technology absorption in the sector is very low. Weaving in India is highly biased towards cotton; the share however has been decreasing at a steady rate over the past few years.
- **Composite Mills:** The competition from the Powerloom sector has seen the share of the Mill sector in weaving to be reduced to insignificant number. The utilisation levels of the mill sector has been declining over the years. Facing a losing battle, the composite mills have been forced to look at exports. Very few have kept pace with technology and use technology to improve on their product and service offer.
- Presence of large number of players in each of the sectors, none of whom are large enough to stimulate demand, has led to a situation wherein the industry as a

whole cannot compete effectively or counter the onslaught from other countries in the international markets. In addition, the industry is passing through a rough phase on account of unabated escalation in the cost of raw materials and power, sluggish market conditions both at home and abroad, slack export performance ever since the South East Asian currency turmoil, rising imports of textile products.

On the rebound, the textiles industry in India has seen significant investments across the supply chain over the last five years; with India strengthening its position as a preferred supply base for a versatile mix of cotton and blended fabrics.

The Nahar: A Profile

Background and Historical Perspective

If there is one thing that distinguishes the Oswals from the country's other business family, it is only gut – feel. This has kept them afloat even after six successive splits. 85 years ago, an 11-year-old boy left his village in search of livelihood. Over a period of time he created a business empire of over Rs.2000 crores. Lala Vidya Sagar Oswal (96) was studying in the 4th standard when he lost his father to plague, which had spread in the area at that time. He was the eldest son in the family. He decided to move out to Ludhiana. There he started an *arthiya* shop and then a provisions store.

However, he suffered losses in both ventures. Ultimately he took up a job on a monthly salary of Rs. 10 with Faqir Chand, a leading hosiery manufacturer of his time, with an assurance that he would be allowed to learn the technicalities of the job. The entrepreneur in him was always alive and vibrant and he picked up the nuances of the trade.

His mother helped him by selling all her jewellery. He installed a machine and started manufacturing socks. The business kept on growing, and in a span of a few years he installed 10 more machines.

"Textile runs in our blood," says Jawaharlal Oswal, 57, the chairman of the Rs. 1800 crores group. Starting in the early 1930's with one sock-knitting unit in a rented room in Ludhiana, Vidya Sagar Oswal along with his brother Lachman Das and Rattan Chand built a textile empire that today is under various family factions. Nahar a separate group is also the result of the second generation family split in 1993 when Jawhar Lal with his two sons Kamal Oswal and Dinesh Oswal broke away from his father Vidya Sagar, and took away the group's choicest companies :**Oswal Woolen Mills, Oswal Fats and Oils, Punjab Concast, Nahar Spinning, Nahar fibers and Nahar exports.**

The Oswal brothers built a textile empire that today, under the various family factions, accounts for in more than Rs. 5000 crore. By the time Jawahar Lal separated, the group had already been through five splits, and the companies that came Jawahar Lal's way had very small textile capacity. Although the companies were totting up Rs.425 crore in sales, the lack of yarn capacities was disturbing the second-generation scion.

What Management of NAHAR group thinks

As we step in to the threshold of the new millennium, its

time to look back, to move forward. Take stock of the past scrutinise our present before chatting our agenda for the future.

Globalisation and liberalisation have opened up a brave new world for us, offering new challenges along with new opportunities. At Nahar keeping pace with the changing environment is our fort since the world is our market and the spirit of excellence, our enduring credo.

Propelled by new technologies and inspired by our exalted goal to explore New frontiers our march towards blazing new trails to span new horizons takes on a new dimension setting the tone for a new millennium.

Jawahar Lal Oswal
Chairman

Vision is the key. Without vision there can be no mission, no agenda to road map the future. Vision provides the vital differential between the ordinary and extra ordinary, defying the cutting edge that powers organisations way above and beyond competition. no progressive group can ignore this vital this.

Kamal Oswal
Director

Globalisation offers exciting challenges that can be converted into rewarding opportunities only if you are sharply attuned to he ground realities pertaining to business and industry. At the end of the day, words remain words. Explanations remain promises. Only performance speaks.

Dinesh Oswal
Director

Incorporation and Integration

Started with just 800 spindles in 1949, the infrastructure of the company today includes a base of 6 factories, manned by 3000 workers Morphing from a Rs 17 million company in 1965 to a Rs 1750 million conglomerate OWM has indeed come a long way from those early factory days. It has also received the honor of becoming the first Indian exporter of woolen garments to Russia .Now the company has set up its own wool combing unit, the first of it's many forward looking, backward integration measures.

FAMILY HIREARCHY OF VIDYA SAGAR OSWAL

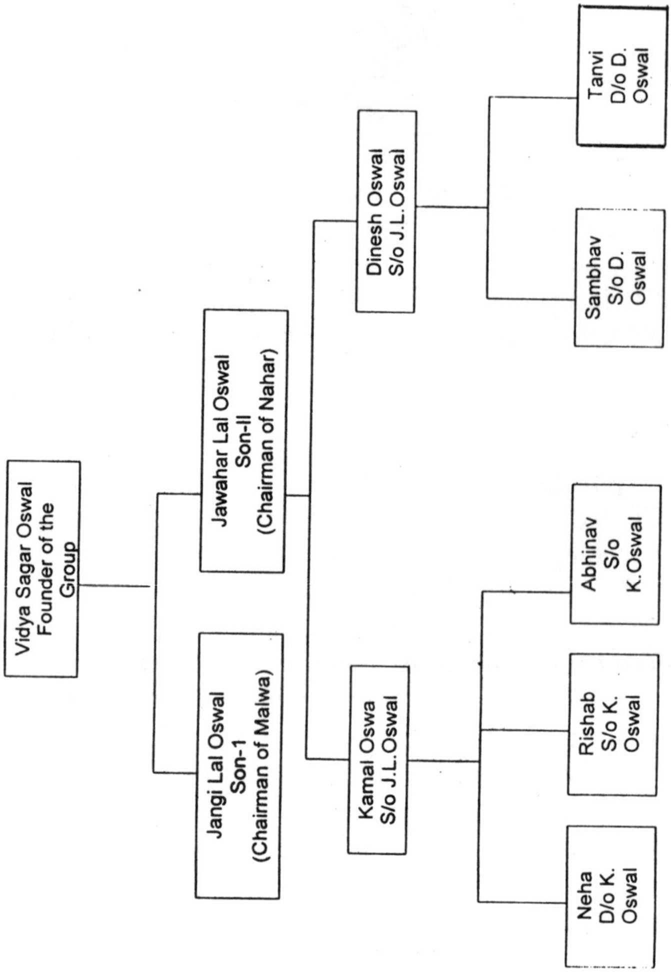

Nahar group is a diversified group. The Group includes the following industrial companies:

Oswal Woolen Mills Ltd.

OWM with over 17200 spindlages is a flagship company, covering product range that is truly large and varied.

From 1949 when small hosiery factory was incorporated into a Public Limited Company, to the present day, constant upward growth has symbolized the charter of a company called Oswal Woollen Mills Limited. From starting out with 800 spindles to 17200 spindles today, from simple hosiery items to high value – added items like designer knitwear, from a turnover of Rs. 165 lacs in 1965 to Rs. 181 crores in the year ended 31.3.2000 – all these are no mean achievements, and what made them possible in so short a time is nothing but a miracle that combined brilliant market insight with diversification, Says Mr. J.L. Oswal, Chairman of the Group

As the company progressively increased spindlage to 2000 in the year 1960, it had already established a market for itself in the areas of hosiery knitwear & textile fabrics like blankets and shawls etc. Very soon, it became the first Indian exporter of woollen garments to Russia and shortly after in 1972, the company set up its OWM Wool combing Unit – the first of several backward integration measures. Soon began the in – house processing for the Woollen Division.

For the domestic market the company launched 'MONTE CARLO', the first truly international range of designer knitwear followed by another prestigious brand "CANTERBURY" Recently an ultra modern Lambs wool &

Angora Spinning plant has been set up, of which more than 50% manufacturer is for captive consumption. The balance meets the requirements of other hosiery knitwear exporters in India. This in turn means immense saving in foreign exchange for India. Further a modernisation cum balancing programme has been introduced to upgrade its capacity for manufacturing garments & fabrics for various Government & Defence departments.

Product Range: Woolen Acrylic and Synthetic blended yarn, Lambs wool yarn, woolen viscose and acrylic tops, and textile fabrics, Woolen hosiery knitwear and cotton garments.

Achievements: Owners of celebrated brands **MONTE CARLO AND CANTERBURY, OWM** is proud recipient of the **"Best Exhibited Product"** award from the International Wool Secretariat for these two glamorous brands. In view of strong brand loyalty enjoyed by Monte Carlo brand, the company has recently introduced a range of premium quality t-shirts under the **Monte Carlo** brand which received a tremendous response

Nahar Spinning Mills Ltd.

Starting out as a tiny worsted spinning and hosiery unit in Ludhiana, it was incorporated as a Pvt. Ltd Company in 1983. Spinning a web of pure enchantment seems to be the aim and objective of Nahar Spinning, reckoned to be the blue chip company in the Nahar firmament

Nahar spinning has 5 plants with nearly 95000 spindles & a wide range of products, over 60% of which is aimed at export market USA, UK, France, Netherlands, Japan, Canada, Korea, Taiwan, Honkong, Singapore, Egypt and Russia. Today, Nahar Spinning T-Shirts are exported to reputed International brands such as Gap, Arrow, Reebock, Old Navy, Pierre Carden, Philips van etc.

Because of it's contribution to Exports, the Company has earned the recognition as an "Export House" followed by a "Recognized trading house", by the Govt. of India. The latest is the prestigious status of "Golden Trading House", in recognition of it's continuously outstanding performance, accorded by the Govt. of India.

With total turnover of Rs 3372 million and net profit of Rs 268 million, Nahar Spinning surges ahead moving from strength to strength.

Nahar International Ltd

Incorporated in 1970, it camc undcr thc management of OWM group in 1980 & was given its present name in 1994, Nahar international Ltd. It has 3 manufacturing units,

a) Punjab con cast steels: Located at Ludhiana, the steel unit of the company is engaged in the manufacture of steel ingots, Billets, Rolled products, steel castings, cast iron castings, Oxygen and Nitrogen Gas. The unit currently manufactures a wide range of products in length and medium sections in various grades of Alloy steel, spring steel, plain carbon stccl, in IS, DIN, En scrics.

b) Arham Spinning Mills: Consolidating on the case strength of the group, the spinning unit of the company, located at Bhiwadi (Rajasthan) is engaged in manufacturing of cotton and blended yarn, commercial production of which commenced in 1993. The installed capacity of the unit at present is 66264 spindles.

c) Arham Spinning mills (100% EOU): The spinning unit of the Company a 100%, EOU-has been set up in Distt. Patiala, Punjab, for the manufacture of cotton/-blended yarn with a capacity of 25200 spindles.

Nahar Exports Ltd.

Nahar Exports started out in 1988 as manufacturers and exporters of cotton garments and knitwear. The company focused on backward integration that is why it set up it's own spinning unit with an installed capacity of 25,000 spindles aiming to provide premium, value added yarn to the market. The company has been honored with the prestigious National export award for outstanding performance (1997) and also with the Trophy by the textile Export Promotion Council for outstanding export performance in yarn amongst the leading exporter mills (1997-98).

An ISO 9002 Company Nahar exports has 5 plants with a spindlage capacity of 145000 spindles and achieved a turnover of Rs 4170 million in the year 1999-2000, Manpower of the company includes 5000 employee and customers are in the competitive market of Europe, Hong Kong, Singapore, Mauritius and South East Asian Countries.

Nahar Sugar and Allied Industries

Established in 1993, Nahar Sugar was promoted by Nahar spinning mills Ltd. and associated companies in the joint sector with PSIDC.

The company has modern sugar mills powered with the latest state of art equipment at district Fategarh Sahib, Punjab for producing all types and grades of sugar and allied products. The installed capacity of the mill is 2500 TCDS.

An active programme of cane development to ensure regular cane supply to plant is on. Also, the power co-generated at the plant is being constructively used for captive consumption to reduce raw material cost.

Nahar Industrial Enterprises

Established in 1983 under the name of Oswal Fats and Oil, It underwent a total change over to become Nahar Industries Enterprise a decade later in 1994.

The Company has two divisions under its umbrella, namely oil and soap division and textile division. The oil and soap division has two units. The fatty acids unit is engaged in the manufacture of fatty acids, stearic acid and distilled glycerin. The soap unit is engaged in the production of toilet and laundry soap. In the textile division the company has spinning units and weaving unit. The first spinning unit, a100%EOU is engaged in the manufacture of cotton yarn. It is exports its yarn to Europe, Hong Kong & Taiwan. The second unit named, Sambhav Spinning Mills, is engaged in manufacture of cotton yarn.

Oswal Cotton Mills

It is located at Lalru, near Chandigarh and engaged in finishing and processing of gray fabrics for bottom wears and shirting having installed capacity of 100000 meters per day. With state of the art equipment, procured from the best source in the world, Oswal cotton mills offers finishing in micro sending, wrinkle free, water repellency, flame retardant, perfumes etc.

Awards and Certifications

An ISO 9002 Company

Best Exhibited Product Award from International Wool Secretariat

Award of Golden Trading House by Govt. of India

Nahar Exports Ltd., part of the Rs 2,000 crore OWM/Nahar Group, has won the coveted Gold Trophy for highest exports of cotton yarn in quota category and Silver Trophy for second highest exports of cotton yarn as manufacturer exporters for the year 2000-01.

Products/Services

Name of the Company	Year of Start	Main Product/Operation	Location of Plants
Oswal Woollen Mills Ltd.	1949	Woollen, Acrylic & Synthetic Blended Yarns, Lambs Wool Yarn, Woollen Viscoseand Acrylic Tops, Textile Fabricswoolen Hosiery Knitwears And Cotton Garments.	G.T. Road, Sherpur, Ludhiana

Nahar Spinning Mills Ltd.	1980	Manufacture And Export Of Woollen /Cotton Hosiery Knitwears &Woollen Textiles	373,Industrial Area-A (Ldh)
Nahar International Ltd. a) Punjab Con-Cast Steels b) Arham Spinning Mills c) Arham Spinning Mills. 100% Eou	1970	A) Steel Ignots, Billets, Rolled Products, Steel Casting.Oxygen & Nitrogen Gas B) Manufacture of Cotton And Blended Yarns C) Manufacture of Cotton And Blended Yarns	A) Focal Point, (Ldh) b) Bhiwindi, Rajastan C) Distt.Patiala (Pb.)

Nahar Exports Ltd.	1988	Exporters Of Cotton Hosiery Garments, Also Set Up Own Spinning Unit.	Ludhiana, Lalru, Sangrur
Nahar Industrial Enterprises Ltd. A) Oil And Soap Division B) Textile Division	1983	 A) Fatty Acids, Stearic Acid And Distilled Glycerine. B) Cotton Yarn	Focal Point, Ldh. Village Mundian.
Nahar Sugar And Allied Industries Ltd.	1993	All Grades Of Sugar And Allied Products	Fategarh Sahib, Punjab
Oswal Cotton Mills Ltd.	1999	Trousers, Shirts, Jacketsand Other Apperal Articles	Focal Point, Ldh.
E Textile Point.Com Ltd.		Textile Related Information	Focal Point, Ldh.

Foreign/Domestic Market Presence

S. No.	Name of the firm	Spindlage (nos.)	Market
1	Oswal woollen Mills ltd.	17,200	Domestic& foreign
2	Arham Spinning Mills	66,264	Domestic
3	Arham Spinning Mills 100% EOU	25,200	Foreign
4	Nahar exports ltd.	1,45,000	Foreign
5	Nahar industrial Enterprises ltd.	38,000	Foreign

Data Sheet

Year of start	1930 Then group split took place in 1993
Main Products/Operations	Yarn, Steel, Hosiery, Acids, Sugar and allied products, Trosures, T-Shirts, Jackets
Total Turnover	Rs. 2000 crores approx.
Domestic Turnover	Rs. 1600 crores approx.
Foreign Turnover	Rs. 400 crores approx.
Certifications	ISO 9002 Best Exhibited Product Award from IWS Best Export House Award
Stock Exchange Listings	Ludhiana Stock Exchange
New Ventures	Nil
Major collaborations	Nil
Flagship company	OWM
Famous Brands	Monte Carlo & Canterbury
Main markets being served: Domestic Foreign	 All over India Europe, Hong Kong, Taïwan, Mauritius and South East Asian Countries.

12

Ralson India Limited

Introduction

The global village exists. Whether we like it or not, whether we want it that way or not, we are in an age of practically instant communication from anywhere to everywhere. The successful corporations of this century will be those who make a decision to join the global business battle and get in touch with what the best-practice global companies are doing right now. The orientation of the global economy has shifted from production to marketing.

The post 1991 scenario, in which the Indian industries are free to breathe in the global environment, has posed a number of challenges before the local industrial houses. In the presence of high tax rates, bureaucratic control and poor infrastructure, the home industry finds it tough to face global competition. This holds good for the Indian Bicycle industry, which is facing intense price competition from the Chinese bicycles. This in turn affects the local tyre and tubes manufacturing companies.

Indian bicycle industry started when East India Company came to Calcutta. It was at that time that the English people brought bicycle and cycle tyre/tube technology to India. At that time, bicycle parts were imported, assembled and marketed in India. In 1953, the scenario entirely changed, when some of the noted companies like Hero and Avon were given licenses to manufacture bicycles.

Today, the cycle industry has grown to a production level of 10 million cycles a year and is growing at the rate of 11 per cent per annum. This in turn has a backward linkage with the tyre manufacturing industry.

Ralson India Ltd. : A Profile

Background/Historical Perspective

Mr. O.P. Pahwa & Mr. S.P. Pahwa started Ralson. Mr. O.P. Pahwa handled the operations of Ralson (India) Limited, Ludhiana until 1991. After his death his son Sanjeev Pahwa became Managing Director of the company.

Ralson: Born in 1974

(O.P. Pahwa and S.P. Pahwa)

|

Separation in 1991

Ralson (India) Limited Ludhiana (Sanjeev Pahwa s/o O.P. Pahwa) ⟷ Ralson Enterprises Limited (S.P. Pahwa)

Both of them have defined their territories in which they will market their products. Ralson (India) Limited has confined its' area of operations to eastern and central India, Goa and Nepal. Whereas Ralson Enterprises Limited operates in western, northern and southern India. When the separated companies have to sell their product in their own areas/territories they do it under the name of Ralson (India) Limited. But when the Ludhiana unit has to sell its' product in the territory of Bhopal unit, the product is sold under the name of Ralson Enterprises Limited. When the Bhopal unit has to sell its product in the territory of Ludhiana unit it uses the name Nosler Enterprises Limited to avoid unhealthy competition.

Incorporation and Integration

Ralson India Limited, Ludhiana was started way back in

the year 1974 by Sh. S.P. Pahwa. Along with his brother Late Sh. O.P. Pahwa, he made the first successful attempt to indigenously manufacture bicycle tyres in India. With the passage of time Ralson grew at an outstanding pace. It not only led the domestic tyre market but also got a break in international markets like South Asia, Latin America, Africa and the Middle East. Today Ralson(India) Ltd. is headed by Mr. Sanjeev Pahwa s/o Mr. O.P. Pahwa, the present managing director of the company. He is a highly focused person who stresses on quality work and has a passion for perfection.

The strength of Ralson lies in its 4000 strong skilled work-force striving zealously to meet their targets . Ralson is the first and only ISO 9002 certified company in the cycle tyre segment in India. It produces cycle tyres and tubes of international standards.

Ralson's daily production is 1,00,500 tyre/tube sets. Such strengths give Ralson an unmatched capability to offer the largest and most comprehensive range of cycle tyre profiles and sizes in India. There are a large number of companies producing cycle tyres like, Usha, Hindustan, Bedrock, Sawhneys, Krishna, etc. Out of all these companies, Ralson (India) Ltd. clearly stands out a winner in quality. The proactive R&D wing of Ralson gives it unmatched capability to custom make tyres, tubes and components for the home and overseas buyers. It also offers an inbuilt guarantee of timely supplies. Perhaps this is why all prominent Indian bicycle manufacturers, like Hero, Avon, Atlas and BSA prefer Ralson tyres and tubes as original equipment in their bicycles.

Ralson has a network of 27 branches across the country.

Awards/Certifications

- Ralson was the first to get R&D recognition from department of Science & Technology, Govt. of India.
- First company to introduce nylon tyres in India.
- First company to make cycle tubes conforming to ISI specifications.
- For three years in succession the Chemical and Allied products Standards Promotion Council of India has conferred upon Ralson the CAPEXIL award for highest export of bicycle tyres and tubes.
- For four consecutive years Ralson has got Comp exel award in exports from Export Promotion Council. It has got ISO 9002 certification on tyres and tubes.

Quality Policy

At Ralson (India) Limited, the workforce is committed to achieve and sustain market leadership through satisfaction of customer's need by continuous improvement in quality, delivery and value for money of their product namely tyres and tubes.

The group proposes to achieve its quality objective by:

- Manufacturing products as per specification and standards agreed with the customers
- Continuously improving the quality of material, processes and products.
- Maintaining and continuously upgrading the quality management system.
- Ensuring active involvement of employees at all levels.
- Creating a safe, healthy, and pollution free working environment.

Competitors

Company Name	Market Share (All Over India)
Ralson	30%
Metro	35%
Govind	15%
Hindustan	15-20%

Products/Services

Ralson started with accessories in 1971
Started manufacturing tyres in 1974
Started manufacturing hubs in 1974
Started manufacturing tubes with jointed tubes in 1982
Started manufacturing nylon tyres in 1983
Started manufacturing cycle nylon in 1990
Started manufacturing bicycle tubes in 1996
Launch of super-shakti tyres in 2000
Launch of R-777 in 2001.

Important Brands of Tyres and Tubes Manufactured by Ralson

Tyres
R-777
Super-Shakti
Diamond Supreme
Himalaya
Ruf-tuf
7 Star
Nylon Grip
Super Master
Punjab Tiger

Tubes
Chetak
Diamond Supreme
Punjab Tiger
Gem
Super-Shakti
Butyl Tubes
Various other ranges

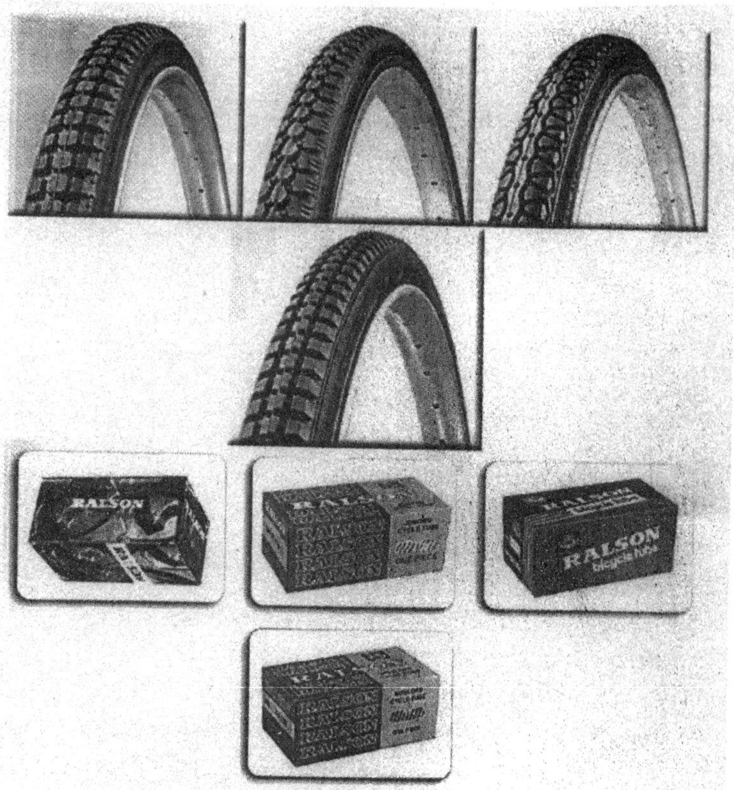

Face to Face with Mr. B.S. Sra
General Manager (Marketing)

The main competitors of Ralson (India) Ltd. are Govind Rubber and Metro Tyres. Still the company maintains the No. 1 position in India and No. 3 in the world in the cycle tyre industry. Ralson exports its products in markets across 51 countries, namely, USA, Africa, Latin America, Mid-East, South-East Asia and Europe. It was able to capture these markets because of it's competitive edge in research and development and technology.

For 4 consecutive years Ralson has got Comp Exel

award in exports from Export Promotion Council. It has got ISO 9002 certification on tyres and tubes from ISI.

Ralson (India) Ltd. has ventured into the business of auto parts. A plant has been established at Doraha for the production of automobile tyres mainly for mopeds and scooters.

The success of the business is attributed to Sh. Sant P. Pahwa and Late Sh. O.P. Pahwa who started the business in the year 1974. The initial production of the company was approximately 300 tyres per day. Today, the production has risen to 1,05,000 tyres per day, 25000 hubs with 4000 workers. The annual turnover of the company is more than 350 crores. The company believes in providing the best quality at reasonable price.

The company believes that human resources are the most critical element in an organisation. The success of any functional department depends on how efficiently the human resources of that department work. That is why Ralson takes care of each and every need of it's workforce and employees. The work environment of the company is highly congenial and acts as a motivational factor to improve the workers' performance.

Mr. Sra said that Indian firms are not able to compete with their foreign counterparts due to existence of undesirable taxation structure. Sales tax imposed on cycle and rickshaw tyres is equivalent to the sales tax imposed on the automobile tyres. On top of it the tax rates vary from one state to another. As cycle and rickshaw tyres are items of use by the common man, tax rates on these items should be minimal.

Presently, they have no future plans of venturing in new fields due to presence of tough conditions in the home market.

Ralson has fully computerised and automated it's operations. They are making use of SAP & ERP in their business. The company's management believes in adoption of the changing technology to keep itself ahead of others in this competitive era.

The management of Ralson never misses an opportunity to serve society. From time to time various camps are organised by the company to uplift the health and hygiene in the society. Service to the society is one of the most important objective of the company.

Ralson gains it's strength from quality production, adaptability to the changing environment, adequate infrastructure and quality equipments sourced from abroad.

Mr. Sra opined that management education provided by the regional institutes should be more practical oriented, with focus on decision making process and case studies. It should help a student to develop analytical skills.

Ralson is on top in the cycle tyre industry today and its management is determined to retain this top position in the coming ten years or more.

Data Sheet

Year of start	1974
Main Products	Bicycle Tyres & Tubes, Cycle mudguards, freewheels, Bells, Seats
Total Turnover	US $ 80 million (as per Website)
Domestic Turnover	20%
Foreign Turnover	80%
Certifications	ISO 9002 CAPEXIL
Stock Exchange Listings	Nil
New Ventures	Auto Tyres at Doraha
Major collaborations	Nil
Flagship company	Ralson India
Main markets being served: Domestic Foreign	 All over India, Goa Nepal 32 branches in the various countries of Africa, Gulf, Latin America, Europe, USA and South Asia.

13

Shreyans Group

Introduction

India has a very rich history in textiles. The trade in Indian textiles is very ancient. We spun the best yarn to clad our women folk. Not only did India provide textiles of immaculate weave but it practised fine art of dyeing and printing. By the first century AD India was already producing woven cottons of noteworthy quality. The world had accepted the Indian contribution in the field of textiles. As the time passed, the industry lost innovation and direction to suit the changing needs. Can we now think of reviving our pre-eminent position and regain our rightful pride place in the world map of textiles?

Recently we have entered into new millennium. With promise of greater globalisation and liberalisation, Indian textile industry seems to be looking ahead with both trepidation and anticipation. How the major structural changes in world economy will affect the prospects of Indian Textiles Industry?

Some of the questions that are going to be posed to the industry include:

- What is the unfolding emerging scenario for Indian textile industry as competition intensifies?
- What are the opportunities and obstacles faced by Indian textile manufacturers?
- How are the expectations of consumers from textiles?
- Is the Indian Textile Industry is geared up for the future?

A review of Indian textile scenario in particular and the world situation in general will help all sectors of Indian

Textile Industry to re-organise themselves to face new challenges both known and unknown that may come in future.

On January 1st, 1974, the Arrangement Regarding the International Trade in Textiles, otherwise known as the MFA (Multi-Fibre Agreement) came into force. It superseded all existing arrangements that had been governing trade in cotton textiles since 1961. The MFA sought to achieve the expansion of trade, the reduction of barriers to trade and the progressive liberalisation of world trade in textile products, while at the same time ensuring the orderly and equitable development of this trade and avoidance of disruptive effects in individual markets and on individual lines of production in both importing and exporting countries. Though it was supposed to be a short-term arrangement to enable the adjustment of the industry to a free trade regime, the MFA was extended in 1974, 1982, 1986, 1991, and 1992. Because of the quotas allotted, the MFA resulted in a regular shift of production from quota restricted countries to less restricted ones as soon as the quotas began to cause problems for the traders in importing countries. The first three extensions of the MFA, instead of liberalising the trade in textiles and clothing, further intensified restrictions on imports, specifically affecting the developing country exporters of the textile and clothing products. Increased usage of several MFA measures tended to further erode the trust which developing countries had originally placed in the MFA.

Under the MFA, product coverage was extended to include textiles and clothing made of wool and man-made fibres (MMF), as well as cotton and blends thereof. With regard to applications of safeguard measures, import restrictions could be imposed unilaterally in a situation of actual market disruption in the absence of a mutually agreed situation. However, in situations involving a real risk of market disruption only bilateral restraint agreements were possible. The Textile Surveillance Body (TSB) was set up to monitor disputes regarding actions taken in response to market disruptions.

Unsatisfactory experience with several extension protocols of the MFA, retention clauses, such as "good will", "exceptional cases", and "anti-surge" and other trade related factors led the developing countries to press for the inclusion of the textile issue in the agenda of the GATT Ministerial meeting.

The eventual outcome of prolonged negotiations was the Agreement on Textiles and Clothing.

Agreement on Textiles and Clothing (ATC)

The ATC calls for a progressive phasing out of all the MFA restrictions and other discriminatory measures in a period of 10 years. In contrast to the MFA, the ATC is applicable to all members of the WTO.

Top 10 Exporters (Textile)

Top 10 Exporters (Textile)
Hong Kong
China
South Korea
Germany
Italy
Taiwan
USA
France
Belgium-Luxembourg
Japan

Post-MFA/ATC Scenario

It is generally believed that quota phase-out can only be beneficial for the industry. In 1993, a study of seven countries found that the price of cotton yarn per kilo, was cheapest in India at US$ 2.79, compared to US$ 3.30 in Brazil, US$ 4.19 in Japan, and US$ 3.10 in Thailand. This was because overall labour and raw material costs are cheaper in India.

However, it should be realised that the opposite can also happen. Removal of quotas may open new frontiers but will also close captive markets. The EU and the US will no longer be restrained in buying as much as they want from the cheapest possible sources. Some argue that the ending of quotas will result in cut-throat competition between developing countries. Coupled with this is erosion in the growth of markets in industrial countries. Apparent consumption of textile products, in real terms, remained stagnant during the decade 1985-95. Purchases become discretionary and fashion-driven. As a result, fashion cycles got shorter and order-cycles compressed. Retailers order requirements on short-order cycle term and demand rapid responses to in-season ordering. Hence, they are compelled to secure their supplies of top-up orders from those in close vicinity.

There is, therefore, a propensity towards sourcing from low-cost countries in the neighbourhood as also a growth of offshore processing by manufacturers in developed countries. Regional integration reinforces this.

Further exporters in India fear that freer imports could lead to dumping of low-cost fabrics from China and other Southeast Asian countries. Thus, the industry needs restructuring on all fronts. Although the policy framework can be blamed partially for its ills, internal factors are equally important.

Recent studies indicate that India is beginning to lose out to its rivals. In one survey of US textile and apparel imports, China and Hong Kong had higher market shares than India. In certain categories, other Asian low cost producers like Pakistan and Indonesia had higher market shares and had emerged as close competitors to India. Because many of these countries depend on imports, however, India can take advantage of home production.

Given India's high quota growth rates during the phase-out period, its competitive product niches and established links with retailers and importers in developed countries, it should experience vigorous growth in the future. The World Bank predicts a growth rate of 16% per annum in the coming decade.

Ultimately, the extent that India will benefit from trade liberalisation depends on its current cost competitiveness, its ability to increase productivity and upgrade quality.

India needs to invest in research and development to develop new products, reduce transaction costs, reduce per unit costs, and finally, improve its raw material base. India needs to move from the lower-end markets to middle level value-for-money markets and export high value-added products of international standard. Thus the industry should diversify in design to ensure quality output and technological advancement.

The weakest links in the entire chain are the powerlooms and the processing houses. The latter especially are very important because they are responsible for the highest value addition in the manufacturing line. A powerloom co-operative structure could be evolved for pooling of common services and functions such as quality testing, marketing, short-term financing, etc. Further, because of the geographical proximity enjoyed, a cluster approach can be adopted.

The government also needs to make policy changes like dereserving the small-scale sector so that it can achieve economies of scale and adopt a synergistic approach.

Handlooms by their very nature can adopt a strategy of "niche" marketing. In this respect, export promotion, common credit and marketing facilities and more significantly publicity are important areas for co-operation. Here too, a co-operative structure would be useful though government agencies should be involved because of their outreach. Newer and more innovative forms of involvement are required where decentralisation should be a key element.

India has made little attempt to forge partnerships – in equity, technology and distribution in overseas markets. The newer nuances of global apparel trade demand joint control of brand positioning, distributing and quality assurance systems.

The Indian textile industry has recognised the need for a cradle-to-grave approach when tackling environmental issues i.e. eco prescription should be applied right from the stage of cultivation to spinning to weaving to chemical processing to packaging. Here especially there is great scope for private -public partnerships.

A great deal of work has been done by Indian trade and industry to comply with ecological and environmental regulations, and so Indian garments can adopt an appropriate label signifying a distinct quality.

Efficiency and output of handloom and powerloom sectors also needs to be increased. The clothing sector needs the support of high quality and cost-effective cloth processing facilities. Modernisation of mills is a must.

Human resource is another area of focus. The workforce must be trained and oriented towards high productivity.

The business environment of the future will be intensely competitive. Countries will want their own interests to be safeguarded. As tariffs tumble, non-tariff barriers will be adopted. New consumer demands and expectations coupled with new techniques in the market will add a new dimension. E-commerce will unleash new possibilities. This will demand a new mindset to eliminate wastes, delays, and avoidable transaction costs. Effective entrepreneur-friendly institutional support will need to be extended by the Government, business and umbrella organisations.

The Shreyans: Profile

Background/Historical Perspective

The Shreyans group was formed in 1987 as the outcome of the restructuring of the business. In 1990, the Company set up another spinning unit of cotton yarn "Shreyans Spinning Mills". The name of Shreyans paper Mills Ltd. was changed to Shreyans Industries Ltd. on Oct.20, 1992. Then onwards the Shreyans Industries Ltd. had two units namely Shreyans Paper Mills and Shree Rishab Paper.

The group has interests in textiles, paper and finance. Dynamic and moderate Mr. D.K. Oswal, a doyen in the cotton spinning industry chairs the group. Mr. D.K. has more than 30 years of experience in the textiles industry. He was previously MD of Vardhman Spinning for 22 years. Mr. Rajneesh Oswal, the eldest son of Mr. DK Oswal has 7 years of techno- commercial experience and at present holds the position of Vice Chairman of the Shreyans group. The promoters of the group belong to the well–known Oswal family of Ludhiana.

Relational Hierarchy of Family Members Involved in Business

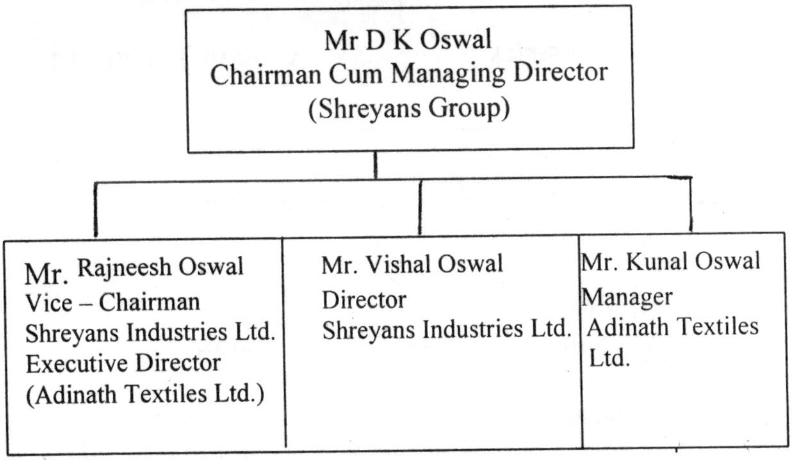

Incorporation and Integration

The group came into existence in the year 1987. Mr.D.K. Oswal took over charge of the Shreyans Paper Mills Ltd. and Adinath Textiles. The initial investment made was Rs.6 crores. The group initially focused on Paper and Textiles and had a turnover of Rs. 2.7 crores. The group has high presence and good potential in the papers and textiles industry with well-set manufacturing facilities. The group has in its fold three manufacturing set ups

Mission

Shreyans aims to be a top class paper and textiles organization producing diverse range of products for the global paper and textiles market. Shreyans seek to achieve customer satisfaction through excellence in quality and customer service. Shreyans is committed to be a responsible corporate citizen.

Shreyans Group

- **Shreyans Industries**
  - **Shreyans Papers**
  - **Shree Rishab Papers**
- **Adinath Textiles Ltd**

Quality Policy

When Quality Leads Productivity Follows

Group Philosophy for Growth

The shreyans group has always striven to be in step with the changing times. It believes in a process of continuous transformation to face the emerging challenges of market led domestic economy and global economic integration. The group has been on a steady growth path and is building competitive strength in products, processes, markets and people for sustainable growth in the coming years.

Future Plans

Shreyans group has plans in the near future for capacity enhancement in both its paper plants. Horizontal expansion is planned through setting-up facility for manufacture of office stationery. Converting plant for maplitho & copier paper. Plans are on the anvil to diversify into information technology sector by going into call centres, medical transcription, software exports, etc.

Major Operating Companies in the Group

Company	Year of Commencing Commercial Operation	Activity/Product	Present Capacity
Shreyans Industries Ltd. (Shreyans Paper Mills Ltd.)	1979	• Cream Wove • Coloured Paper • Duplicating Paper • Maplitho Paper • Offset Paper • Super Printing Paper	30,000 Tons Per Annum
Shreyans Rishabh Paper	1994	• Cream Wove • Surface Sized Printing Paper • Maplitho Paper • Offset Paper • Rail Ticket Paper	25,000 Tons Per Annum
Adinath Textiles Ltd.	1987	• Hand Knitting Yarn • Fancy Yarn • Machine Knitting Yarn • Carpet Yarn in Acrylic	34,000 Metric Tons Per Annum

Technology Sharing

Shreyans group is looking for technology up gradation and technology sharing in the following areas on global basis.

- Improvement in quality of pulp (Agro based)
- Improvement in quality of paper (Agro based)
- Water Management system (in agro based Paper units)

Business Alliances

The Shreyans group is also looking for business alliances both in domestic and international market for export of paper from 50 GSM to 170 GSM in Africa, Middle East and South America.

Shreyans Paper Mills Limited

Shreyans Paper Mills limited was established in the year 1979 with Mr D. K. Oswal as the Chairman. The initial investment made in the unit was Rs. 6,00,00,000 with 40% of equity, 55% borrowing, and 25% subsidy. It was the first of two paper units in the fold of Shreyans group. It has a production capacity of 75 tons per day. The turnover (both domestic and exports) of this unit is Rs.150 crores. Writing and Printing paper is manufactured here. It utilises residue like straw, wheat straw and sugarcane residue there by converting waste into wealth. Its product i.e. Paper, is being sold all over India through a dealer network.

Soda Recovery Plant

Raw Material Handling

The unit has received several productivity and quality awards over the past 10 years. It has received prestigious National Productivity Council Award for three consecutive years in 1988, 1989 and 1990. It has received the best consumer service award in 1987. This award being contributing silently to the conservation of our precious forests reserves. The group is totally domestic with no foreign collaboration.

The R &D section is equipped with ultra modern equipments to ensure quality products to its valuable customers. R&D lab equipped with lad Digester, Lab valley

Beater Brightness, opacity and gloss testing Machine, Burst strength tester, Double Folding Endurance Tester, Gurley, Porosity, smcothness tester and Cobb Tester. State of art automation system Valmet Qxd 9000, installed from Valmet (Canada) to keep Strict Control on ash contents, Grammage variation and moisture percentage to produce quality papers. The unit also has the rare distinction of being the only unit, which was installed under US ATD test program. Due to the success of this technology at Shreyans papers and a commitment to clean environment, the same plant was also installed at Shree Rishab Papers, and is running successfully. The main competitors of this unit are Varinder Agromills, Ludhiana, and ABC Paper Mills, Hoshiarpur. The unit is listed on all major stock exchanges of India. Its stock is listed on Ludhiana, Mumbai, Kolkata, Madras, Ahemdabad and Delhi stock exchanges.

Shree Rishab Papers Limited

It is an agro-based unit of Shreyans Group located in village Babah, Distt. Nawanshehar. Shreyans group took over this unit from Birla Zenith Papers mills, a unit of Zenith Ltd., in the year 1994. This unit is presently known as Shree Rishab Papers. It has a product profile similar to that of Shreyans Paper Mills Ltd. It is a similar unit having an annual capacity of 25,000 M.T. The Unit is supplying its products to Indian Railways, Postal department, Universities and educational boards throughout India. The Unit has excellent technology inputs and parameters in the industry. The Unit also has state-of-art automation system measures 2002 EL (ABB), installed from ABB, to have strict control over ash contents, grammage variation and moisture % contents to produce quality papers.

The main competitors of the company in India are Varinder Agromills, Ludhiana and ABC Paper Mills Hoshiarpur. Its products are marketed all over India through a network of dealers. Its product enjoy a substantial market share. The Company is listed on all major stock exchanges of India, i.e., Ludhiana, Mumbai, Kolkata, Madras, Ahmedabad and Delhi.

Adinath Textiles Limited

Adinath Textiles Limited, based at Ludhiana is the largest worsted-spinning unit in the Indian subcontinent, with an installed capacity of 12,000 spindles for manufacturing the hand knitting yarn, fancy yarn, machine knitting yarns and carpet yarn, in Acrylic with vast variety to meet every type of count combination demanded by of its prospective customers. Equipped with the latest technology imported from Italy, France and Belgium the group products exemplify unwavering commitment to total quality. The raw material used in the company is both imported and indigenous fibers.

The unit is catering to domestic market in the hosiery sector and hand-knitting sector. Although its products find customer all over world, these are specifically marketed in Northern India consisting of Punjab, Himachal Pradesh, Chandigarh, Delhi, and, in the international market it finds customer in Bangladesh, SAARC Countries, Hong Kong, etc. Adinath is also catering to the export market and is presently exporting mainly to Bangladesh, Hong Kong and Middle East markets. The Unit has latest R&D equipment to keep strict quality control at various levels of production. Annual capacity of the plant is 34,000 M.T. The lists of competitors include Vardhman Spinning & General Mills, Malwa Cotton & Spinning Mills, Punjab Worsted Mills, Anshupati Mills and other Ludhiana Based Mills. The total turnover from the unit is Rs. 29.94 crores. It is listed on Ludhiana, Mumbai, Delhi, Calcutta, Madras and Ahmedabad stock exchanges.

Products/Services

Shreyans Paper Mills

Cream Wove
Coloured Paper
Duplicating Paper
Surface Sized Printing Paper
Azure Laid Paper
Maplitho Paper
Stamp Paper
Inland Letter Paper
Postal Envelope Paper
Offset Paper
Cover Paper
Super Calendered Paper
Rail Ticket Paper
Super Printing Paper

Shree Rishab Paper Mills

Cream Wove
Coloured Paper
Duplicating Paper
Surface Sized Printing Paper
Azure Laid Paper
Maplitho Paper
Stamp Paper
Inland Letter Paper
Postal Envelope Paper
Offset Paper
Cover Paper
Super Calendered Paper
Rail Ticket Paper
Super Printing Paper

Foreign Presence

Imports of the Group

Acrylic Fiber	3 Denier	Bright, Vcl, Raw White, Tow, Fiber
Acrylic Fiber	3 Denier	Bright, Dyed Tow
Polyester Fiber	3 Denier	Bright, Vcl, Raw White& Dyed
Polyester Fiber	10&20 Denier	Trilobal, Vcl, Raw white
Nylon Fiber	6,7,10,30, Denier	Super Bright, Vcl, Raw White
Cationic Dyes	100%strength or more	Looking for competitive suppliers from China and other countries
Dispersed Dyes	100%strength or more	Looking for competitive suppliers from China and other countries

Face to Face with Mr. D.K. Oswal
Chairman & Managing Director

The group attributes the success of its business to dedicated efforts, hard work and team spirit.

When asked to comment on the criticality of human resources as compared to other functional areas, Mr. Oswal expressed the opinion that Human Resources should be given prominent significance over and above the other resources, since this is the only resource which has emotion and whose productivity may be affected due to many factors and which in turn may affect the productivity of other resources. He believes that it is only this resource, which makes use of other resources, and thus this resource has always been given pivotal importance in the group policy framework.

Commenting on Ludhiana industry, he was of the belief that Ludhiana Industry was mature enough and had the capability to meet any challenge. In the past also, after USSR division it was able to look after other European and USA market and today too it has developed a very good reputation in new markets. However, the thing that mattered the most was that Ludhiana industry looked at the State Government for providing better opportunity and environment free from Babu Raj. Mr. Oswal was confident that Ludhiana Industry has a bright future and already it has got a very good name in world's cycle and garment industry.

The group was of the opinion that Indian firms had the gut power not only to face the global competitiveness but also had the capability to excel and make their presence felt. This fact was well established by India when Indian IT industry became the world's most sought after industry and today all countries were looking on India for supply of well-trained manpower. In engineering industry also India had made its presence well accepted in the world industry. Mr. Oswal believed that the time was not far away when India would be a super power in the world.

Since the group had been successfully working in the

paper industry, it was looking for future ventures in this area for both forward and backward integration of the present production facilities. The group was also thinking of venturing into technology transfer on turnkey basis in the area of continuous raw material feeding and chemical recovery fields where they had experienced manpower to handle such projects.

In the present scenario IT had made the global business possible on a very high scale, and distance and location boundaries had almost vanished. In order to benefit from this sector, the group was also looking for suitable ERP software to be implemented.

Shreyans is a responsible corporate, it wishes to play a very positive role in its social commitment and to develop on a continuous basis various social welfare scheme for the community. They have set in a chemical recovery plant and plan to do much more for the community.

Shreyans are pioneers in few fields, e.g., as it is the first company which had a recovery plant installed in the Paper Mill. Further it enjoys good image in the industry as quality wise it is leading in the market with 70 % of supply of its product to the government department.

Regarding management education provided by educational institutes, the Oswals believe that with the opening up of economy and global competition, the management education had gained importance. Earlier there were only a few institutes such as PAU, which were providing qualified manpower, but with liberalisation in the education field many new institutions have come up with good facilities. Mr. Oswal is of the opinion that Punjab College of Technical Education is one such institute which is doing fairly well in the education field.

The group visualizes itself to be India's No.1 Paper

conglomerate in the coming years. Further it believes that it has an edge in the field of technology transfer. Mr. Oswal strongly believes that they would definitely make it to the top position.

Registered Offices

Shreyans Group's
Village: Bholapur
P.O. Sahabana
Chandigarh Road
Ludhiana 141123
Punjab, India
Tel.: +91 161 2604149 to 2604151, 301082, 2604123 - 25
Fax: +91 161 2604148
E-mail: adinath.ldh@smx.sril.net.in

Shree Rishab Papers
Village: Banah
Nawanshaher (144522)
Punjab (India)
Tel.: +91 1881 73627 to 73629
Fax: +91 1881 73645
E-mail: shreyans.srp@smx.sril.net.in

Shreyans Papers
Village: Malikpur
Ahmedgarh 148021
Punjab (India)
Tel.: +91 167 3640347 to 349
Fax: +91 167 3640512
E- mail: Shreyans.ahmd@smx.sril.net.in

Adinath Textile Ltd.

Village: Bholapur
P.O.Sahabana
Chandigarh road
Ludhiana 141123
Punjab (India)
Tel.: +91 161 2604149 to 2604151
Fax: +91 161 604148
E- mail adhinath.ldh@smx.sril.net.in

Branches

Mumbai Office
302, Raheja Chambers

New Delhi Office
4E,Gopala Towers

Name and Designation of the Main Employees of the Division

Shreyans Paper Mills

1. Mr. D K Oswal Chairman-cum-Managing Director
2. Mr. Ranjneesh Oswal Vice Chairman
3. Mr. Anil Kumar Executive Director
4. Mr. S K Sharma Technical Director

Shree Rishab Paper Mills

5. Mr. D K Oswal Chairman-cum-Managing Director
6. Mr. Ranjneesh Oswal Vice Chairman
7. Mr. Anil Kumar Executive Director
8. Mr. S K Sharma Technical Director
10. Mr. Raman Marwaha General Manager and Unit Head

Adinath Textiles Limited

Mr. Ranjneesh Oswal Executive Director

14

Upper India Steels

Introduction

Iron and Steel industry in India is over 125 years old. India is the tenth largest producer of crude steel in the world with production of 24 million tonnes and investment of Rs.1,000 billion. The country produced 23.82 million tonnes finished steel in 1998-99, compared to a meager one million tonne in 1947. In the year 1999-2000 it produced 26.48 million tonnes of Finished Steel showing an increase of 11.16 per cent against the previous year.

The first steel plant was set up by Iron Work Company at Kulti in 1870. However, large scale production got underway only when the Tata Iron and Steel Company (TISCO) was set up at Jamshedpur in 1907. The Indian Iron and Steel Company (IISCO) was set up at Burnpur in 1919. The first unit in the public sector, now known as Visveswaraya Iron & Steel Limited (VISL) began production at Bhadravati in 1923. After Independence, three integrated steel plants were set up in the public sector at Bhilai, Durgapur and Rourkela with one million tonne capacity. Later two more public sector integrated steel plants came up at Bokaro and Visakhapatnam and several steel units in the private sector.

The public sector Steel Authority of India (SAIL) with five integrated steel plants at Bhilai, Bokaro, Durgapur, Rourkela and Burnpur (run by IISCO, the subsidiary of SAIL) is the largest producer of steel in India and eleventh largest in the world. SAIL has four Alloy Steel and Ferro-alloys units at Durgapur, Salem, Chandrapur (run by SAIL subsidiary Maharashtra Electrosmelt Ltd.) and Bhadravati (run by SAIL subsidiary Visveswaraya Iron & Steel Limited). Together with Visakhapatnam Steel Plant of Rashtriya Ispat Nigam Limited (RINL) another public sector company, the public sector accounts for a major portion of the total production. The balance is produced by the private sector, mainly by TISCO, the oldest steel plant in the country. The private sector, which was producing 7.4 million tonnes of finished steel with market share of 51.4 per cent in 1991-92 has been playing a major role in steel production.

The health of the iron and steel industry is linked with the economic condition of the nation. The general slow down of the economy and some other factors like dumping from the CIS and South East Asian countries in the last two years, has adversely affected the Indian steel industry. However, with the expected growth rate of the economy, led by large-scale investments in infrastructure and housing sectors, the iron and steel sector has shown growth. The production of finished steel has gone up by 12 per cent during 1999-2000 compared to 1998-99 while that of pig iron increased by 5 per cent and sponge iron by 2 per cent.

The export performance of the Indian steel industry was very good during 1999-2000. Exports of finished steel increased by almost 51 per cent to 2.6 million tonnes while exports of pig iron increased to 2.9 million tonnes. International prices have started firming up, and this would ensure the continued presence of Indian steel in the global markets. Exports are also expected to take care of the increased supply of some finished steel products especially from the new producers in the country. Domestic steel prices have also firmed up in line with the international markets. This is expected to improve the bottom line of the major steel producers in the country. In the first quarter of year

2000-01, the steel sector has kept up its tempo of production and export of the last quarter of 1999-2000.

India's present per capita consumption of crude steel is only 24 kg. which is very low compared to the developed and developing countries – 422 kg. in USA, 417 kg. in Germany, 109 kg. in Russia and 87 kg. in China. Our consumption is less than 1/5th of the world average i.e. 121 kg. Government of India has taken a number of steps to boost up the per capita consumption of steel in the country.

Until the 1990s, the iron and steel sector was by and large the exclusive preserve of only the public sector, the sole exception being TISCO. The new economic policy announced in 1991 was a significant mile stone which brought out a sea change in Indian iron and steel industry. In the post-liberalisation era, the structure of the steel industry underwent a sea change with the advent of major steel producers in the private sector with world class technologies and capacities. Many all India financial institutions came forward to support the private initiatives by sanctioning financial assistance to 19 steel projects involving an investment of about Rs.30,000 crore to create an additional capacity of 13 million tonnes (mt.) per annum. Today India is the 10th largest steel producer in the world producing 27.82 million tonnes of finished steel a year. The industry represents nearly Rs.9,000 crore of capital and directly provides employment to over 0.5 million people. The world's largest producer of steel is China (107 mt.) followed by Japan (104 mt.) and USA (97 mt.)

Due to slow down in steel industry in the world, many steel companies in India incurred losses after 1997-98. The giant PSU, SAIL made a loss of Rs 1574 crore. The government recently has approved a financial and business restructuring package for SAIL involving a massive waiver of Rs.5073 crore from Steel Development Fund and Rs.381 crore from the Government of India. The other measures in the package include provision of Government guarantee for Rs. 3000 crore to be raised by SAIL for its VRS and to meet its repayment obligations on past loans. SAIL has been asked in the package to initiate process of divestment in some non-core assets protecting jobs of its existing employees. With the Government initiative, the mining lease for the Kudramukh Iron Ore project has been renewed for a year and steps are being taken to get 20 years lease. The government also approved a second capital restructuring package for RINL in May 1998 converting Rs.133.47 crore in preferential capital. The company has also prepared a turn-around plan to get out of its financial difficulties.

The government has been making all possible efforts to help the domestic steel industry to overcome their problems. To boost the demand and consumption of steel, an Institution for Steel Development and Growth (INSDAG) has been set up involving the leading steel producers in the country. The Development Commissioner for Iron and Steel had launched a national campaign for increasing the demand for steel in the non-traditional sectors, particularly in the construction, rural and agro-based industrial sectors. Other areas include reduction in power and railway tariffs, reduction in input costs, strengthening of anti-dumping mechanism, setting up a steel exporters forum and an empowered committee for research and development.

Background/Historical Perspective

Upper India Steel (UIS) is not a story of a Mini Steel Plant. It is a vision to pioneer a collective human effort with one goal in mind, **"TO BE THE BEST"**.

It was in 1965 when Mr. Inder Mohan Singh Grewal, a

man with clear vision founded a team of entrepreneurs having the technical knowledge of esteemed institution and expertise to pioneer production of special and alloy steel. Better known as **"STEEL MAN OF PUNJAB" – I.M.S. GREWAL, CMD, UIS** is assisted in accomplishment of his goal by his brothers.

Since the first batch of ingots rolled out over nearly four decades ago on April 13th 1965 technical development being of prime concern, UIS expanded its capacity periodically from its meagre 6000 TPA to its ever growing current capacity of 200000 TPA in 2000-2001. The constant Research and Development at UIS ensures its endeavour for the finest quality product. This is why perhaps UIS may be amongst the only Indian outfit to fully adopt the **ZERO DEFECT CULTURE.** This concept is an operational philosophy that promotes the conscious and constant desire to do a job "Right the First Time." Moving on this path UIS has achieved an important milestone by implementing International Quality Standards ISO 9002.

UIS has always sought to continuously adapt itself to changing environment and customer needs and new evolving technologies. With a view to meet the growing demand for high quality steel from specific customer – users, it is progressively developing and upgrading its plant and machinery through the installation of modern equipment for meeting "Customer's Changing Needs." As a result, it has achieved remarkable progress within a period of thirty-five years from a small turnover of Rs. 0.946 Cr. in 1965-66 to a turnover of Rs. 120 Cr. by the end of 1999-2000 financial year.

Incorporation and Integration

Upper India Steel Manufacturing and Engineering Company Was Founded In Year 1965. The company is spread over an area of 36 acres with lush green lawns. The high standards, both in expertise and result oriented endeavours, have sustained a successful history of producing high quality products from its very inception. UIS represents the country's commitment to progress through self-sufficiency, professional experience, and utilisation of proven expertise and adoption of welfare environment in order to produce a wide range of high quality steels in India. UIS excels in producing Spring Steel, Forging Quality Steel catering primarily to the OEM's in the automotive sector. In the Tool Segment, UIS is the largest producer of which is exported finally the world over, earning foreign exchange for the country. With a zero strike rate UIS boasts of an exceptional approach to management at all levels. Constant exchange of ideas and welfare schemes keep the physical, emotional and psychological parameters at their best. UIS employs hundreds of persons belonging to different faiths and religions. The company is a shining example of *"Unity in diversity."*

At a mammoth cost, anti air pollution equipment with Japanese technology has been installed to ensure a dust free environment.

UIS has an advanced Steel Melting Shop with system standardisation of the highest degree enabling it to cast a wide range of high quality steels cost effectively. UIS has numerous rolling mills interwoven together, enabling it to roll a wide array of sections simultaneously, at short lead times, and working towards the JIT concept.

The constant Research & Development at UIS ensures its endeavour for the finest quality products. This perhaps is why UIS may be amongst the only Indian outfit to fully adopt the **Zero Defect** culture. Moving on this path the company has achieved an important milestone by implementing International Quality System Standard ISO 9002.

UIS has made forays into the international markets in the File Steel sector of which it is the largest manufacturer in the country. UIS is a regular exporter to Spain, Mexico and Columbia. Various functions of UIS comprising of purchase, inventory, sales, finance and personnel are knitted together with state of the art information flow systems, using local area networks.

Markets: Foreign Presence and Domestic Presence

The main markets served by UIS are:

➢ **Domestic Market:**

1. OEM's (Original equipment manufacturers):
   a. Automobile manufacturers
   b. Vendors of automobile manufacturers.
2. Replacement Markets.
3. Engineering / Tools Industry.

➢ **International Market:**

UIS exports FILE STEEL to Mexico, Columbia and Spain for Chisel work, SPECIAL STEEL FLATS to Nepal and Saudi Arabia. UIS is also making indirect exports to USA, UK, Europe, Australia, Gulf Countries and Bangladesh etc. through Export Agencies / Traders / Manufacturers.

Competitors of UIS:

The major competitors of UIS are: -

1. Sunflag Iron and Steel Co. (Nagpur)
2. Modern Steels (Mandi Gobindgarh)
3. Vardhman Special Steel (Ludhiana)
4. Punjab Concast (Ludhiana)

5. Aarti Steels (Ludhiana)
6. Bhushan Steels (Chandigarh)
7. Mukand Steel (Mumbai)
8. Usha Martin (Bihar)

Future Plans of UIS

The future plans of UIS are to add up:

- 22" Fully automatic rolling mill.
- Cold drawing facility.
- Vacuum Degassing facility.

Products / Services

UIS represents the country's commitment to progress through self-sufficiency professional experience, utilisation of proven expertise and adoption of welfare environment in order to produce a wide range of high quality steel in India.

UIS excels in producing Spring Steel, Forging Quality Steels catering to the OEM's in automotive sector. In tools segment UIS is the largest producer of File Steel nation-wide most of which is exported finally the world over.

Various Kinds of Steel Manufactured in the UIS:-

- Carbon Steel
- Carbon – Manganese
- Alloy Steel
- Semi / Free Cutting Steel
- Boron Steel
- Spring Steel (Silico Manganese and Chrome Vanadium Moly Steel)
- File Steel
- Cold Forging Quality Steel

ORGANISATION CHART

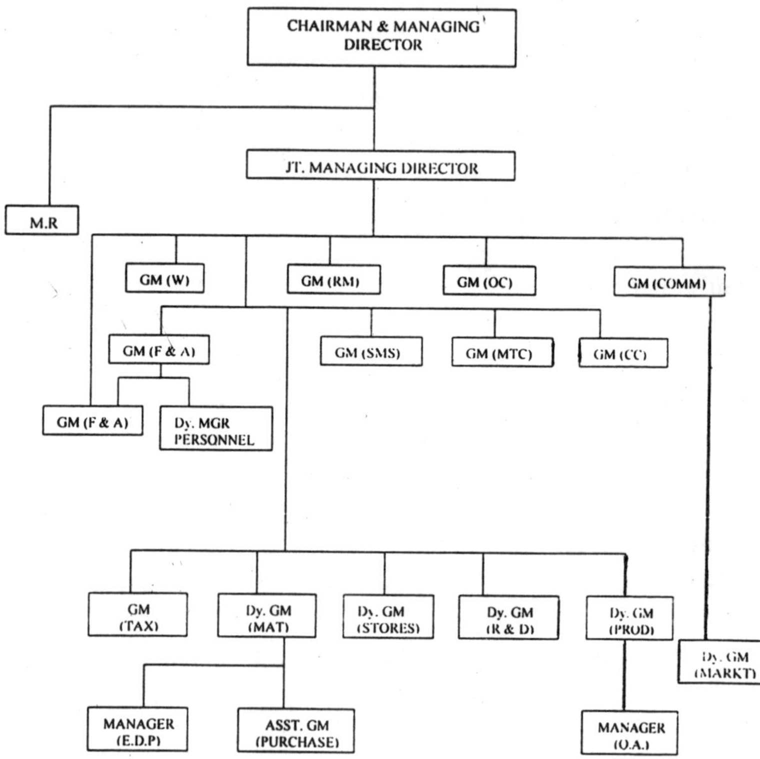

For the steel manufactured in the company, the following grades stand for:

EN: British Standard

SAE: American Standard

AISI: American Standard

SUP: Japanese Standard

Data Sheet

Year of Start	1965
Main Products	Steel
Total Turnover	Rs. 125 crores (approx.)
Domestic Turnover	60%
Foreign Turnover	40%
Certificates	ISO: 9002
Stock Exchange Listings	Nil
New Ventures	Nil
Major Collaborations	Nil
Flagship Company	Upper India Steel

15

Vardhman

Introduction: Cotton Spinning Sector

The delicensing of spindelage in 1991 provided an impetus to the growth of the cotton spinning sector in terms of capacity. Spindelage has since been rising steadily. There was an approx. 35% growth in the number of installed spindles in 1991, to approximately 35 million in 2001. However, the spinning industry could not benefit from the expanded capacity due to adverse global factors like Southeast Asian crisis, worldwide economic slowdown, and increased costs. The phenomenal rise in raw cotton prices in the 1994-95 season added another dimension to the economies of the spinning sector.

All these were reflected in stagnant production in the four years up to 1998-99. A revival has been witnessed in 2000-01. To sustain this revival certain issues need to be addressed. A major effort is needed to reduce the cost of production. The cost of almost all components—power, raw material, transport and labour —has gone up during the past four or five years leading to high cost of production. Power needs to be provided to the industry at international cost. This will go a long way to help increase India's share in the global cotton yarn market. There is also a need to increase productivity to meet international competition.

Rationalization and relief of excise duty is one factor that can assist in revival of this sector. Good quality yarn needs to be made available to the domestic sector as well so that this sector can add to the demand. This sector needs to be 'restructured' to tackle the problems at the factory level and address the external factors affecting this sector.

View of Vardhman Corporate Office at Ludhiana

The Vardhman Group: Profile

Background and Historical Perspective

The 60s...

The decade of the sixties saw the birth of one of today's largest textile-manufacturing group. Lala Rattan Chand Oswal founded Vardhman Spinning and General Mills Ltd at Ludhiana on 7th December 1962. The unit was incorporated on 27th December 1962.VSGML started commercial production of cotton yarn with 6,000 spindles in November 1965.

The 70s...

The Seventies saw the small mill growing into a large conglomerate. In 1975 the unit was granted industrial license for 50,000 spindles. In 1977-78 the unit diversified into Acrylic yarn spinning and became the 1st textile mill in the country to spin acrylic yarn on modified cotton spindles. In the same year 15,000 spindles were diversified into the production of synthetic and blended yarns. It also introduced "Hand knitting Yarns" for the first time, which later became its premium product. This year also witnessed a major diversification in the production programme of VSGM by shifting to manufacture of industrial yarns. In 1980, the first dye house of the group was commissioned for in-house dyeing of yarn and fabric.

The 80s...

Start of the eighties was not auspicious as the industrial unrest caused closure of factory for 3 months from 14th April 1982 to 19th July 1982. In 1984-85, the latest generation G-5 ring frame was installed in Unit-II .In 1985-86, VSGML started exporting cotton yarn to Bulgaria and exports were spread to Western Europe and other parts of the world. In 1987-88, Quality circle movement took birth in VSGML with the inception of Quality Circle "Aradhana" in the dye house. In the last year of this decade, VSGML was awarded with the IBPL Energy Conservation Award.

The 90s...

This decade saw Vardhman emerging as the largest textile producer and exporter of the country. Vardhman received numerous awards in this decade. VSGML was accorded the status of "Recognised Export House" by the government of India on 20th September 1990, on the basis of major export from the unit. Vardhman was awarded the "TEXPROCIL" bronze trophy for excellence in exports in 1992-93. In 1993, VSGML became the first textile mill in the country and the first industrial unit in Punjab to be awarded the prestigious ISO 9002 certification. Shri S.P.

Oswal was awarded Exports Excellence Award by the then President of India, Shri S.D. Sharma on 17th December 1994.The production of dyed yarn product, "Daffodil" commenced in 1994.

The year 1995 saw a major change in the group as the unit was bifurcated into Unit-I involved in manufacture and sale of spun yarn and Unit-II, engaged in dyeing of yarn and related activities on 6th May 1995.

The founder of the Vardhman group, Lala Rattan Chand Oswal passed away on the night of 5th/6th January 1998.

In the year 1998-99, Spinning-2 started the production of polyester sewing thread for the first time. In the last year of the century, 2000, "CUDDLES" India's first ready to knit pack for mothers was launched by Miss India 2000, Gul Panag, on 14th September 2000. "Bunte Bunte Kismat Chamke", a contest for the hand knitting yarn customers was also launched in the same year.

The New Millennium...

The beginning of the new millennium saw ERP [Enterprise Resource Planning] being implemented in VSGML.

History of Setting Up Projects: Company-wise

Vardhman Spinning & General Mills Limited (VSGML)

This flagship company of the Group, was set up in 1962 by the Oswal's, with a capacity of 6000 spindles for manufacturing of cotton yarn at Ludhiana, Punjab. The unit commenced production in 1965. The company has, over the years, expanded the spinning capacity at Ludhiana to reach at present level of installed capacity of 61708 spindles. This unit also has a Dyeing capacity of 18tpd.

Family Tree

Mr. S.P.Oswal
Chairman & MD

Mr. Sachit Jain ED (VSGM) (Head of Baddi Operations)	Mrs. Suchita Jain ED (VSGM & VMT)

In the year 1973 company put up a Mini-steel plant at Faridabad in the name of Oswal steels. Later on in the year 1994-95 company sold out this Steel Unit with a capacity of 25,000 MT per annum of Rolled products to another Group Company, namely M/s Mahavir Spinning Mills Limited.

In order to diversify its operation geographically, in 1989, the company decided to set up a new spinning unit under the name and style of "Auro Spinning Mills" with a capacity of 25,200 spindles in village Baddi, Tehsil Nalagarh, Distt.

Solan, in the state of Himachal Pradesh. The unit became fully operational in 1991. Over the years, the spindleage has increased to 67560 spindles.

VSGML also set up a Weaving Unit at Baddi in March 1992, for manufacture of cotton grey cloth with installed capacity of 72 Looms. Over the years, the number of looms has been increased to 208.

The Company has also set up a dye house at Baddi in technical collaboration with NIHON SANMO, Japan, in 1995 for fibre. yarn dyeing capacity of 18 tpd. Over the years, the capacity has been expanded for yarn dyeing to 8tpd, and for fibre dyeing to 22 tpd

The company set up new 100% Export Oriented Unit (EOU) of 25000 spindles. The unit was commissioned in March 1998. The present capacity of the unit is 27040 spindles.

The company has set up 'Fabric Process House" in the name and style of "AURO TEXTILES" at Baddi with technology from Topai Sanyo, Japan, with final capacity of 30 million metres. The unit was commissioned in 1999.

Mahavir Spinning Mills Limited (MSML)

Mahavir Spinning Mills Limited (MSML) was promoted by M/s Vardhman Spinning & General Mills Limited (VSGM). The company was incorporated in October 1973.

In 1975, the company set up a spinning mill with an installed capacity of 25,000 spindles for manufacturing cotton, synthetic and blended yarns at Distt. Hoshiarpur, in Punjab. The capacity of Hoshiarpur Unit has been steadily increased and is presently at 56,000 spindles.

In 1981, the Company set up a new spinning unit with an installed capacity of 25,000 spindles by the name of Arihant Spinning Mills for manufacturing cotton and acrylic yarns at

Malerkotla, Distt. Sangrur, Punjab. Over the years the Company undertook capacity additions and presently has a capacity of 1,11,892 spindles.

In the same year, i.e., 1981, the Company diversified its product line by setting up facilities for manufacturing of sewing thread with an installed capacity of 4.5 tonnes per day (TPD) at Hoshiarpur, Punjab. The capacity of the aforesaid sewing thread unit has been gradually expanded to 17TPD.

On April 1, 1988, Mohta Industries Ltd., a sick company, was merged with Mahavir Spinning Mills Ltd. As approved by the Board for Industrial and Financial Reconstruction (BIFR). Mohta Industries Ltd., at the time of merger, had a division known as Mohta Alloys & Steel Works, a mini steel plant at Ludhiana. This division is now a part of Mahavir Spinning Mills Ltd. The company has renamed the mini steel plant from Mohta Alloys & Steel Works to Vardhman Special Steels. The company has also set up a Rolling Mill with an installed capacity of 40,000 TPA, in its Ludhiana Steel Unit for manufacture of a wide range of alloy steel/rolled products. The rolling mill has become operational in 1995. The present capacity of SMS is 135000 MT per annum and of rolling products is 65,000 MT per annum.

In the year 1994-95 Company also acquired a Steel Unit of another Group Company, namely M/s Vardhman Spinning & General Mills Limited, which had a rolling Mills facility at Faridabad in the name of Oswal Steels with a capacity of 25,000 MT per annum. This steel division at Faridabad has been non-operational since November 2000.

In 1992, the Company set up a 100% Export Oriented Unit (EOU) for manufacture of cotton yarns with an installed capacity of 25200 spindles under the name and style of Anant Spinning Mills at Mandideep, Distt. Raisen in Madhya Pradesh. Over the years the company undertook different expansion schemes and presently has capacity of 74496 spindles.

The company, in 1994-95, set up a gassed mercerized unit at Hoshiarpur, Punjab in technical collaboration with Kyungbang Ltd., South Korea with a capacity of 1.7 tpd. The capacity of the aforesaid unit has been gradually expanded to about 7.00 TPD.

In the year 1999-2000 the company undertook an expansion of Sewing Thread business by installation of Unit-II at Ludhiana with a capacity of 5 TPD to be implemented in two phases. The first phase with a capacity of 2.5 TPD has commenced production in January 2001.

Vardhman Polytex Limited

VPL was originally promoted in the joint sector by Mohta Industries Limited (MIL) and Punjab State Industrial Development Corporation Limited (PSIDC), & was incorporated in the name of Punjab Mohta Polytex Ltd (PMPL) in August 1980. The spinning unit of the company at Bhatinda, Punjab, started commercial production in 1984 with an installed capacity of 9504 spindles and 504 rotors. In April, 1988 MIL which had been registered with Board for Industrial and Financial Reconstruction (BIFR) as a sick Company, was merged with Mahavir Spinning Mills Limited (MSML), as a consequence VPL also came under the fold of the Vardhman Group. With the acquisition of PSDIC's shareholding by MSML, VPL became a subsidiary of MSML with effect from June 1989. The name of the company was changed from Punjab Mohta Polytex Ltd to Vardhman Polytex Ltd in August 1991. At the time of merger, MIL had a division known as Mohta Alloys & Steel

Works, a mini steel plant at Ludhiana. The division is now a part of MSML.

Vardhman Polytex Limited came out with Right-cum-public issue of Fully Convertible Debentures in February 1993, the conversion of which was due in October 1993. After the said conversion, the Company ceased to be a subsidiary Company of MSML. The capacity of this Unit has been gradually increased to 49472 spindles.

VPL, in 1990 – 91, added a new Worsted Spinning Unit at Ludhiana, under the name of Anshupati Textile, with a capacity of 4800 spindles to manufacture acrylic yarn of various counts. The capacity of the plant stands increased to 8000 spindles.

The Company commissioned a DTA unit at Baddi under the name & style of Arisht Spinning Mills with a capacity of 25000 spindles in 1996 – 97 Presently the installed capacity of the aforesaid unit is 41472 spindles.

Further, the Company commissioned a 100% Export Oriented Unit (EOU), under the name of Arisht Spinning Mills (100% EOU) at Baddi in 1997 – 98 with an installed capacity of 24288 spindles.

Vardhman Threads Limited

In the year 1993 – 94 Mahavir Spinning Mills Limited entered into a Joint Venture Agreement with one of the world's best manufacturer of Industrial Synthetic Threads, M/s Barbour Campbell Group Limited of Ireland. A joint venture company named Barbour Vardhman Threads (Pvt.) Ltd. was incorporated and a plant to manufacture industrial synthetic threads was set up Baddi with an installed capacity of Industrial Sewing Threads of 1TPD. The Company started its commercial production in April 1995. Its products have specialized application for Shoe and Leather Industries.

During the year 1992 – 2000 the management & control of M/s Barbour Campbell Group Limited was taken over by a competitor company, viz Coats Viyella Inc. which made the continuation of Joint Venture practically difficult. Accordingly, in the same year MSML entered into a Disengagement Agreement whereby it bought out the entire stake of 'Barbour Group' in the Company and the JVA stood terminated w.e.f March 2000, thus making the company a 100% subsidiary of MSML. Upon the approval of the members, the company continued its activities under the new name **Vardhman Threads Limited.**

VMT Spinning Company Limited

Mahavir Spinning Mills Ltd. in the year 1994 – 95 entered into a Joint Venture Agreement with M/s. Marubeni Corporation and Toho Rayon Company Limited of Japan for setting up of 100% Export Oriented Unit to Manufacture Cotton Yarn. Production Facility was established at Baddi in Himachal Pradesh by the name of VMT Spinning Company Limited (100% EOU) with an installed capacity of 25000 spindles. This Company has started its commercial production in September 1996. The capacity of the aforesaid unit has been gradually expanded to 28320 spindles.

Vardhman Acrylics Limited

In the year 1994-95 Mahavir Spinning Mills Ltd. signed a Technical Collaboration Agreement with M/s Kawasaki Heavy Industries Limited and Marubeni Corporation for the transfer of technical know-how from the M/s Japan Exlan Company Limited (acrylic fibre manufacturer) for setting up an Acrylic Fibre Project for manufacture of 16500 TPA. Pursuant to Joint Venture Agreement entered by the Company, the Acrylic Fibre Project was set up at Jagadia,

Bharuh by the name and style of Vardhman Acrylics Limited (Subsidiary of Mahavir Spinning Mills Limited). This subsidiary of MSML started its commercial production in March 1999. the present installed capacity of the Company is 16500 MT (TPA).

Incorporation and Integration

The Vardhman Group is one of the largest Textile houses in the country with a turnover of about Rs 1900 crores and employs around 20,000 people. The group has sizeable presence in spinning, weaving, sewing threads, textile processing, acrylic fiber manufacturing and alloy steels.

The Vardhman Group started its corporate journey with installed capacity of 6000 spindles in 1965 under the Flagship Company Vardhman Spinning & General Mills limited at Ludhiana. Over the years the group has expanded its spinning capacities besides adding new business. The group has also diversified yarn processing, weaving, sewing thread, fabric processing, acrylic fiber manufacturing and special and alloy steel.

Sewing Threads: In 1982 Vardhman entered the sewing thread market as a forward integration project. With 53,000 spindles capacity at Hoshiarpur, Vardhman threads are the second largest selling brand in the country.

Fabric: Another integration has been Vardhman's entry into weaving. Grey fabric-weaving division at Baddi has already made its mark as a quality producer in the home market.

Today the Vardhman Group comprises of three listed and three unlisted companies & two joint ventures –

Listed Companies

1. Vardhman Spinning And General Mills Ltd.

2. Vardhman Polytex Ltd.
3. Mahavir Spinning Mills Ltd.

Unlisted Companies

4. Vardhman Threads Ltd.

Joint Ventures

5. Vardhman Marubeni Threads Spinning Co. Ltd.
6. Vardhman Acrylics Limited.

All the three Unlisted Companies are subsidiaries of MSML and were started as Joint Venture with Foreign Partners. As on date VMT & VAL are still Joint Venture Companies where as the group has already bought back the shares in VTL, and VTL has now become a 100% subsidiary of MSML.

Vardhman is a leading group in India having interest in textiles and 'special steel' manufacturing. The group has expanded manifold since its inception. The group has 18 operational plants with installed spinning capacity of about 5,50,000. Spindles, 216 shuttle less looms and about 45 tonnes per day dyeing capacity, capable of Processing variety of raw materials available world-wide.

Vardhman is earning laurels by exporting yarns and fabric of international quality to several countries in the West, Africa and the Far East earning valuable foreign currency for the country. Vardhman is the first company among textile industry to receive the ISO 9002/ISO 1400-quality awards in India.

The uniqueness of the Vardhman group lies in the fact that not only has it excelled in all its endeavours but has also established a firm footing through its deep rooted culture that imparts the group an unassailable strength and confidence to face the future.

Vardhman Group consists of integrated facilities of spinning, weaving and finishing with half a million spindles, weaving capacity of 208 looms and fabric finishing capacity of 30 million metres per annum.

Distribution of Vardhman Products

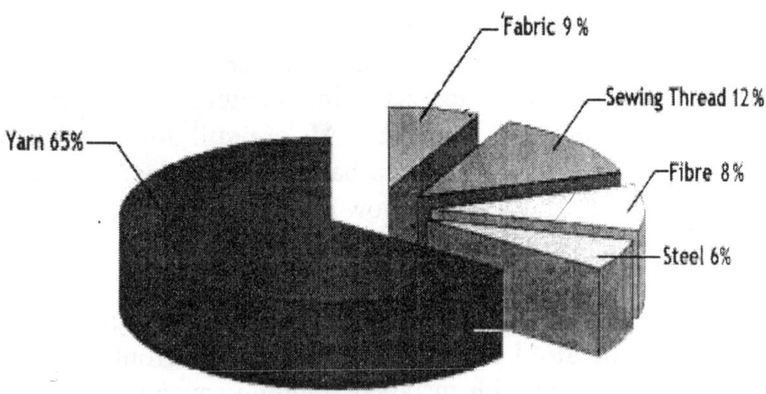

The details of Vardhman group companies comprise of the following:

1. Vardhman Spinning and General Mills, Ltd

Vardhman Group started its operation with a 6000-spindle plant in 1965 under the flagship Company VSGM Ltd at Ludhiana. Presently the company is involved in manufacturing yarn, blended yarn, Acrylic yarn, Hand Knitting yarn, Woven fabric, processed fabric and yarn and fibre dyeing.

Vardhman Spinning and General Mills Ltd, Ludhiana: Mr. S.P. Oswal is the chairman of VSGM, Ludhiana. This unit is serving the domestic market. It has a capacity of 61,000 spindles i.e. of 13 T/day. The product range includes – cotton, blended, acrylic, hand –knitting fancy industrial yarns and yarn dyeing.

Auro Spinning, Baddi: This unit gas a production of 68,000 spindles. This unit also caters to the domestic market. The product range includes cotton, blended, fibre dyed and fine count.

Auro Weaving, Baddi: Auro weaving is also serving the domestic market and it has installed capacity of 216 air jet looms. This unit produces grey woven cotton and blended yarns fabric.

VSGM 100% Export Oriented, Baddi: This is a fully EOU and has capacity of 26,000 spindles. It produces cotton yarn.

Auro Dyeing Mills, Baddi: Auro Dyeing mills situated in Baddi is serving the domestic market. This unit has a capacity of 32 T/day. This unit is into Fibre Dyeing and Yarn Dyeing.

Auro Textiles, Baddi: This unit has a capacity of 85,000 Mtr/day and is serving the domestic market. This unit deals in fabric processing.

Vardhman Spinning and Weaving Unit, Ludhiana (Under raising):

2. Mahavir Spinning Mills, Ltd

This company was promoted by M/s Vardhman Spinning & General Mills Ltd. In the year 1973. The company began its commercial production in the year 1975 at Hoshiarpur with an installed capacity of 25,000 spindles. The company now manufactures Cotton yarn, Blended yarn, Acrylic yarn, Gas mercerized yarn, Sewing thread and Steels.

Mahavir Spinning Mills, Hoshiarpur: This unit is serving the domestic market and has a production capacity of 53,000 spindles for production sewing threads and a capacity of 5 T/day for gas mercerised and dyed yarns.

Arihant Spinning Mills, Malerkotla: It consists of two units. One is EOU with capacity of 21,000 spindles to produce cotton yarns. Other unit is a non EOU with a capacity of 64,000 spindles and the products produced are : cotton, blended, acrylic, mélange, fine count.

Arihant Spinning Mills, Mandideep

Anant Mills, Bhopal

3. Vardhman Polytex Ltd., Bathinda

This Company was originally promoted by Mohta Industries Ltd. & Punjab State Industrial Development Corporation Ltd. In the year 1980 under the name of PMPL. The company started its commercial production in 1984 with an installed capacity of 9504 spindles and 504 rotors at Bathinda. The group acquired the Company in the year 1988. Today Company manufactures Cotton yarn, Blended yarn, and Acrylic yarn.

Vardhman Polytex Ltd., Bathinda: This unit has a capacity of 35,000 spindles and is serving the domestic market. It produces cotton yarn.

Anshupati Textile Mills, Ludhiana: Anshupati Textiles is serving the domestic market. It has an installed capacity of 8000 spindles. This unit deals in Acrylic yarns.

Arisht Spinning Mills, Ludhiana

Arisht Spinning Mills Export Oriented Unit, Baddi: ASM Baddi is a 100% EOU. It has an installed capacity of 24,000 spindles and produces cotton and blended yarn.

4. Vardhman Marubeni Tohorayon (VMT) Spinning Co. Ltd., Baddi

In the year 1994-95 Mahavir Spinning Mills Ltd. entered into another Joint Venture agreement with M/s Marubeni

Corporation & Toho Rayon Co. td. Of Japan for setting up a 100% EOU in Baddi to manufacture cotton yarns with an installed capacity of 25,000 spindles. The company has a capacity of 28320 spindles as on date.

VMT is an EOU with a capacity of 28,000 spindles. It produces cotton yarn.

5. Vardhman Threads, Baddi

In the year 1993-94 Mahavir Spinning Mills Ltd. entered into a joint Venture agreement with M/s Barbour Campbell group of Ireland to manufacture Industrial sewing threads. The manufacturing facility was set up at Baddi with an installed capacity of 1 TPD.

BVTL situated in Baddi is a non-EOU. It has a production capacity of 1 T/day. It deals in core spun polyster and Nylon sewing threads.

6. Vardhman Acrylics Ltd., Bharuch

Thc acrylic fibre unit was set up in the year 1999 at Jaghadia, Bharuch with an installed capacity of 16500 MT (tpa). The Company was promoted by MSML in Joint Venture with Marubeni Corporation, Japan and Japan Exlan Company Ltd., Japan. The technical know-how for the plant was taken from M/s Japan Exlan Company Limited.

This unit is serving the domestic market. It has an installed capacity of 45 T/day. It produces acrylic fibre.

7. Vardhman Special Steels
Vardhman Special Steels, Faridabad.
Vardhman Special Steels, Ludhiana.

The Mission

"Vardhman aims to be a world class textile organisation,

producing diverse range of products for the global textile market. Vardhman seeks to achieve customer delight through excellence in manufacturing and customer service based on creative combination of state-of-the art technology and human resources. Vardhman is committed to be responsible corporate citizen."

- The FLAME signifies growth i.e. growth of each and every individual associated with it whether he/she is a worker, employee, shareholder or customer.
- The STICK symbolises cotton, which is the basic raw material of the core product of Vardhman.
- The "V" stands for Vardhman.

From a small beginning with 6000 spindles in 1965, the group has come a long way to emerge as the largest yarn spinner in the country with a capacity of over half a million spindles. The product range has also expanded from 100% cotton yarns to the largest range of grey and dyed cotton, blended and synthetic yarn. Group has total of twenty manufacturing units spread all over India. Sh. S.P. Oswal, Chairman who is a gold medallist in Master of Commerce, heads the group. He is supported by Professionals/Unit heads and Corporate team. Corporate Office of the Group is situated at Ludhiana where most of the business decisions including Sales/Purchase/Finance/Projects/HRD/ Secretarial are taken. A team of Professionals is there in Corporate Office to support Chairman for carrying out group operation.

Location Map

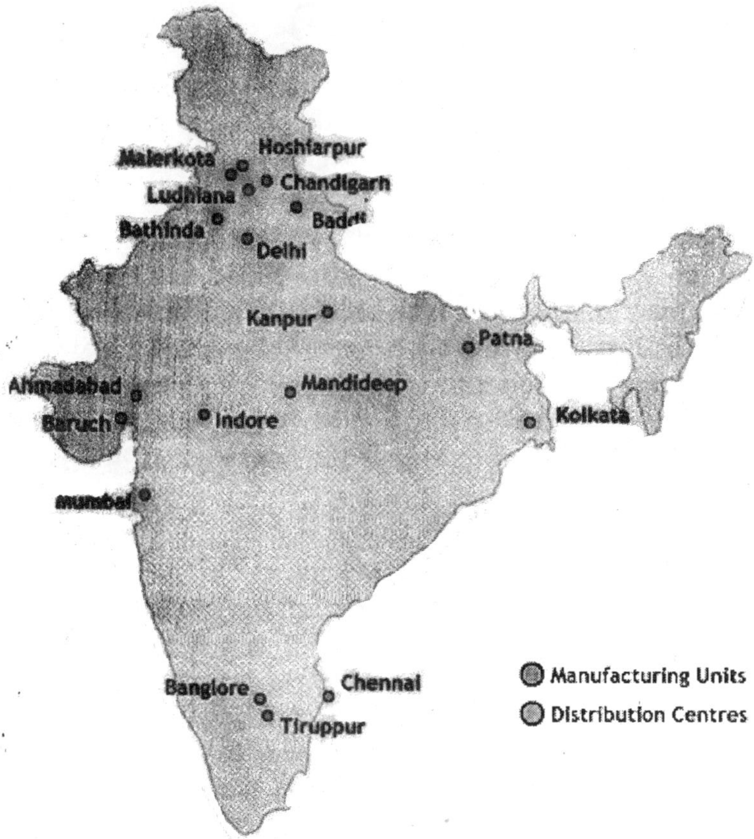

Products/Services

Yarns

The group is the largest spinning group of the country with a spindlage of about 5.5 lakh spindles. The group has twelve production plants located in the states of Punjab, Himachal Pradesh and Madhya Pradesh. In many of the yarn market segments Vardhman holds the position of market leader, besides being large and reliable supplier in the country. Vardhman is also the largest exporter of yarn from India. The group yarn exports amount to over USD 100 million covering the most quality conscious markets in the world. The total export of the cotton yarn of the group is about 7% of total export of cotton yarn from the country.

Sewing Thread

Vardhman entered the sewing thread business in 1982 as a forward integration of its yarn business. The group had to struggle for survival being pitted against the large multinational organizations. Today with approx. 21 MT per day sewing thread manufacturing capacity in its plant at Hoshiarpur, Ludhiana and Baddi. Vardhman threads have emerged as second largest selling sewing thread brand in the country, next only to Madura Coats Ltd.

Weaving

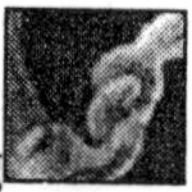

Continuing its onward march on the value curve, Vardhaman group entered weaving business in 1992 with a capacity of 7 million meter per annum. The capacity has been subsequently expanded to 24 million meter per annum.

The group has already made a mark as quality producer of grey poplin / shirting / suiting in the home market and has also entered the highly competitive export market. The group is now exporting a fairly large volume of its production.

Processed Fabric

In its quest for further value addition Vardhman started fabric processing in 1999.Vardhman established a modern fabric process house in 1999 with a capacity of 30 million meters per annum. Vardhman fabric is dedicated to meet customer demand for top quality finished fabric through product innovation, world-class quality, state of art technology and excellence in service.

Fibre

In 1999, the group set up an Acrylic staple fibre plant at Bharuch in Gujarat in collaboration with Marubeni and Japan Exian of Japan. The plant has annual capacity of 165000 mt per annum.

Steel

The steel business was set up in 1973 as diversification with a capacity of 35000 mt per annum. Later on group acquired a steel plant from Mohta group of industries in 1988 and converted this loss making unit into a profitable business in first of operation with the group. Subsequently, the steel mill has been modernized and expanded to a capacity of 100000mt per annum. Catering to high technology quality conscious alloy steel segment, the unit has a reputation of being a dependable source of supply of special and alloy steel to Indian/ International standards.

Name of the Company	Year of Start	Main Prducts(S)/ Operations)	Location
Vardhman Spinning and General Mills Ltd.	1965	Spun Yarn, Fibre Dyeing, Yarn Dyeing, Woven Fabric and Fabric Processing	Ludhian, Punjab
Auro Spinning	1990	Cotton, Blended, Fibre Dyed and Fine Count	Baddi, H.P
Auro Weaving	1992	Grey Woven Cotton and Blended Yarns Fabric	Baddi, H.P
VSGM100% EOU	1997	Cotton Yarns	Baddi, H.P
Auro Dyeing Mills	1995	Fibre Dyeing and Yarn Dyeing	Baddi, H.P
Auto Textiles	2000	Fabric Processing	Baddi H.P
Vardhman Spinning and Weaving Unit- II	Under raising	Yarn Dyeing	Ludhiana Punjab
Mahavir Spinning Mills	1973	Spun Yarn, Sewing Thread, Gassed Mercerization, Steel Melting and Rolled Products	Hoshiar-pur, Punjab
Arihant Spinning Mills	1981	Cotton Yarns, Cotton, Blended, Acrylic, Melange, Fine Count	Maler-kotla, Punjab
Anant Spinning Mills	1992	Cotton Yarn	Man-didee P

Arihant Mills		Cotton, Blended, Melange, Fine Counts	Bhopal, M.P
Vardhman Polytex Ltd	1980	Spun Yarns	Bathinda. Punjab
Anshupati Textile Mills	1990-91	Acrylic Yarns	Ludhiana Punjab
Arisht Spinning Mills	1996-97	Cotton, Blended Yarn	Ludhiana Punjab
ASM Export Oriented	1997-98	Cotton, Blended Yarns	Baddi, H.P
Vardhman Marubeni Threads Spinning Co.	1996	Spun Yarn	Baddi, H.P
Vardhman Threads Ltd.	1995	Industrial Synthetic Thread	Baddi, H.P
Vardhman Acrylics Ltd.	1999	Arylic Staple Fibre	Baruch, Gujarat
Vardhman Special Steels	1973 (closed as on date)	Steel	Farida-bad, Haryana
Vardhman Special Steels	1988	Steel	Ludhiana Punjab
Mahavir Spinning Mills	2001	Sewing Thread	Ludhiana Punjab

Foreign/Domestic Presence

Collaborations

In today's world each and every company needs to work in collaboration with some other company and take advantage of the synergy. Vardhman has also collaborated with the world leaders. The various companies with which Vardhman has collaborated are:

1. Marubeni and Toho Rayon of Japan for VMT Spinning Co. Ltd,

In its growth program through strategic alliances,

Vardhman has streamed its VMT Spinning Co. Ltd. With Toho Rayon, Japan, a pioneer in spinning technology and Marubeni, the worlds largest house in order to service the global market.

2. Nihon-Sanmo Dyeing Ltd., Japan for the Fibre/Yarn dyeing house.

To keep pace with the changing expectations of users, industries and consumers, Vardhman has collaborated with the Nihon-Sanmo Dyeing Ltd., Japan, and the world leaders in dyeing technology, to provide the know-how for its fibre/yarn-dyeing house.

3. Kyung Bang Limited, South Korea for gas mercerized dyeing.

To match the ever-growing needs of the garment manufacturing industry, value addition has been done to the gas mercerized yarn. Vardhman invited technical know-how regarding the dyeing process from Kyung Bang Ltd., South Korea.

4. Marubeni Corporation and Exlan of Japan for Acrylic Fibre Plant.

For the Vardhman's 300-crore Acrylic Fibre Plant, Vardhman has collaborated with the Marubeni Corporation and Exlon of Japan, world famous producer of Acrylic staple fibre, with the best wet spinning technology in the world.

5. Tokai Senko, Japan

Vardhman has collaborated with Tokai Senko of Japan for technical know how of process house. The production capacity would be 50,000 meters per day of processed fabric.

6. A & E, USA

A license agreement for production and marketing of A & E's products in India has recently been signed. This is expected to form the basis of further business between the two companies.

S.No	Name of the firm	Capacity	Market
1	Vardhman Spinning And General Mills, Ludhiana	61,708 Spindles	Domestic
2	Anshupati Textile Mills, Ludhiana	8,000 Spindles	Domestic
3	Mahavir Spinning Mills, Hoshiarpur	56,000 Spindles	Domestic
4	Vardhman Polytex Ltd., Bathinda	49,472 Spindles	Domestic
5	Arihant Spinning Mills, Malerkotla	1,11,892 Spindles	Domestic
6	Auro Spinning, Baddi	67,560 Spindles	Domestic
7	Asm, Baddi	24,288 Spindles	Exports
8	Arisht Spinning Mills, Baddi	41,472 Spindles	Domestic
9	VMT, Baddi	28,320 Spindles	Exports
10	VSGM 100% Eou, Baddi	27,040 Spindles	Exports
11	Arihant Spinning Mills, Malerkotla	21,000 Spindles	Exports
12	Anant Mills, Mandideep	74,496 Spindles	Exports
13	Auro Dyeing, Baddi	30 TPD	
14	Auro Weaving Mills	208 LOOMS	
15	Auro Textiles, Baddi	30 Million mtrs /yr	
16	Vardhman Special Steels, Ludhiana	1,00,000 MTA – Billets 40,000 MTA – Rolling	
17	Vardhman Special Steels, Faridabad	Closed as on date	
18	Gassed & Mercerised Unit, Hoshiarpur	7 TPD	
19	Msml, Ludhiana	2.5 TPD	

Group Business and Capacities

Spinning	5,50,000 Spindles
Weaving208	Air-Jet Looms
Sewing Threads	22 Tonnes/Day
Yarn/Fibre Dyeing	45 Tonnes/Day
Steel SMS	100000 Tonnes/p.a.

Awards and Certifications

The group has so far received 22 awards for excellence in exports from various organizations like TEXPROCIL, FIEO, Punjab Deptt. of Industry. The group has bagged gold trophy from Texprocil six times for being the largest exporter in categories like Yarn and Woven fabric.

Group Company	No. of Awards Won	
VSGM	14	5 Gold Trophies from Texprocil 4 times Best Exporter award from Punjab Department of Industry and FIEO
MSML	7	Gold Trophy from Texprocil and outstanding export performance award from FIEO.
Anant		Gold Trophy

IS 14002/ISO 9002

Certification

Diversification

The first major diversification came in 1973 with the setting up of Oswal steels (later named as Vardhman Special Steels) at Faridabad, to manufacture special and alloy steel with an initial capacity of 50,000 metric tons, along with matching rolling mills and equipped with modern chemical, metallurgical and mechanical laboratories to produce special and alloy steels.

An aerial view of steel plant

In 1986, it added another steel unit, also named Vardhman Special Steels at Faridabad. At present the group has combined steel melting capacity of 1,25,000 tpa and rolling mills capacity of 65,000 tpa. / 20,000 meters per day.

About Shri S.P. Oswal

Mr. S.P. Oswal heads the Vardhman group. Born on 8th April, 1942 at Ludhiana, he joined the family business in 1966 when the group turnover was Rs. 1.5 crores with spinning capacity of 12,000 spindles.

Mr. Oswal did his schooling and Bachelors in commerce at Ludhiana. He obtained Masters in Commerce from Punjab University in 1966.

At present Mr. Oswal is acting as chairman of Vardhman Spinning & General Mills, Ludhiana. He is also acting as executive chairman of Mahavir Spinning Mills Ltd., Ludhiana, chairman and managing director of Vardhman Polytex Ltd., Ludhiana, chairman of Vardhman Agencies Ltd., Bharuch and chairman of VMT Spinning Company Ltd., Baddi.

Apart from these positions he is also a member of Punjab Pollution Control Board, Patiala, Member of National Council, Confederation of Indian Industry (CII) and Chairman of Punjab State Council, Northern region, CII, and member of committee of Administration, TEXPROCIL.

He also has been founder president and director of Ludhiana Stock Exchange Association, Ludhiana, and President Northern India Textile Mills Association. Mr. Oswal also takes keen interest in field of education. He has been a member of Board of Management, Punjab Agricultural University, Ludhiana and Member, Board of Governors, Punjab Technical University, Jalandhar.

Mr. Oswal has one daughter, Ms. Suchita, who is acting as executive director of the group. She is married to Mr. Sachit Jain and he is also acting as the executive director of the group.

Data Sheet

Year of Start	1962
Main Products/Operations	Cotton, Blended, Acrylic, Hand Knitting Yarn Production, Yarn Dyeing And Specialty Steel Production
Total Turnover	1908 Crores
Domestic Turnover	75%
Foreign Turnover	25%
Compound Annual Growth Rate Of Sales For Last 10 Years	14.84
Certificates	ISO 9002
Stock Exchange Listings	Nil
New Ventures	Nil
Major Collaborations	1. Marubeni and Toho Rayon of Japan for VMT Spinning Co. Ltd. 2. Nihon-Sanmo Dyeing Ltd., Japan for the Fibre /Yarn dyeing house. 3. Kyung Bang Limited, South Korea for gas mercerized dyeing. 4. Marubeni Corporation and Exlon of Japan for Acrylic Fibre Plant. 5. Tokai Senko, Japan. 6. A & E, USA.
Flagship Company	VSGM, Ludhiana.
Main Markets Being Served Domestic	All over India.
Foreign	Asia, Middle East, Africa and Europe.

Key People: Vardhman Group

Shri Paul Oswal
Chairman cum Managing Director

Sh. Rajinder Mohan Malla
Nominee of IDBI

Sh. Surinder Kumar Bansal
Nominee of IFCI

Sh. Sachit Jain
Executive Director

Smt. Suchita Jain
Executive Director

Sh. Gopal Krishana Sharma
Company Secretary

Sh. Neeraj Jain
Vice-President

Sh. Mahesh Arora
Vice-President (Mktg)

Col.P.S. Choudhary
Vice-President (HR)

Business Families of Ludhiana

(Critics are the best friends)

Feedback Form

Name: ____

Designation:____

Organization:_______________________________________

Address :____

Phone No.____

Comments:

Contents:____

Presentation:_______________________________________

Coverage:____

Suggestions if Any:

____

____

____

____

____

____

____

____

____

____